Infant/Toddler Caregiving

A Guide to

Culturally Sensitive Care

Edited by
Peter L. Mangione

Developed collaboratively by
WestEd

and

California Department of Education

with funding from
Carnegie Corporation of New York

the Program
for
infant
toddler
caregivers

Publishing Information

Infant/Toddler Caregiving: A Guide to Culturally Sensitive Care was developed by WestEd, San Francisco. See the Acknowledgments on page vi for the names of those who made significant contributions to this document.

This publication was edited by Sheila Bruton, working in cooperation with Peter L. Mangione, WestEd, and Mary Smithberger, Consultant, Child Development Division, California Department of Education. It was designed and prepared for photo-offset production by the staff of CDE Press, with the cover and interior design created and prepared by Paul Lee. Typesetting was done by Carey Johnson.

It was published by the Department of Education, 721 Capitol Mall, Sacramento, California (mailing address: P.O. Box 944272, Sacramento, CA 94244-2720). It was printed by the Office of State Publishing and distributed under the provisions of the Library Distribution Act and *Government Code* Section 11096.

ISBN 0-8011-1057-2

Ordering Information

Copies of this publication are available for $12.50 each, plus shipping and handling charges. California residents are charged sales tax. Orders may be sent to California Department of Education, CDE Press, Sales Office, P.O. Box 271, Sacramento, CA 95812-0271; FAX (916) 323-0823. Mail orders must be accompanied by a check (payable to California Department of Education), a purchase order, or a credit card number, including expiration date (VISA or MasterCard only). Purchase orders without checks are accepted from governmental agencies only. Telephone orders will be accepted toll-free (1-800-995-4099) for credit card purchases only.

In addition, an illustrated catalog describing publications, videos, and other instructional media available from the Department can be obtained without charge by writing to the address given above or by calling the Sales Office at (916) 445-1260.

Photo Credits

The California Department of Education gratefully acknowledges Sheila Signer for the use of the photos that appear in this publication.

Notice

The guidance in *Infant/Toddler Caregiving: A Guide to Culturally Sensitive Care* is not binding on local educational agencies or other entities. Except for the statutes, regulations, and court decisions that are referenced herein, this handbook is exemplary, and compliance with it is not mandatory. (See *Education Code* Section 33308.5)

Prepared for printing
by CSEA members

Contents

Preface

At a time when half the mothers in the United States are gainfully employed, most of them full time, more young children require care outside the home than ever before. The growth of child care services has failed to keep pace with the rapidly increasing demand, making appropriate care for young children difficult for families to find. Training is needed to increase the number of quality child care programs, yet the traditional systems for training child care providers are overburdened. In response to this crisis, the California Department of Education's Child Development Division and WestEd have collaborated to develop an innovative and comprehensive approach to training infant and toddler caregivers called The Program for Infant/Toddler Caregivers. The program is a comprehensive training system featuring a document entitled *Visions for Infant/Toddler Care: Guidelines for Professional Caregiving,* an annotated guide to media training materials for caregivers, a series of training videotapes, and a series of caregiver guides.

The purpose of the caregiver guides is to offer information based on current theory, research, and practice to caregivers in both centers and family child care homes. Each guide addresses an area of infant development and care, covering major issues of concern and related practical considerations. The guides are intended to be used hand in hand with the program's series of videos; the videos illustrate key concepts and caregiving techniques for a specific area of care, and the guides provide extensive and in-depth coverage of a topic.

This guide was written by noted experts in the field of culture and early childhood education. Like the other guides in the series, this one is rich in practical guidelines and suggestions. The information and ideas presented in this document focus on how caregivers can support the early development of infants and toddlers in their care by becoming sensitive to the vital role in that development of the children's home culture and language.

J. RONALD LALLY
Director
WestEd

DELAINE EASTIN
State Superintendent of Public Instruction

ROBERT A. CERVANTES
Director
Child Development Division

JANET POOLE
Administrator
Professional Development Unit
Child Development Division

Acknowledgments

This publication was developed by WestEd under the direction of J. Ronald Lally. Funding for this document was generously provided by the Carnegie Corporation of New York. Special thanks go to Jesus Cortez, Louise Derman-Sparks, Janet Gonzalez-Mena, Alicia F. Lieberman, Peter Mangione, Jayanthi Mistry, Carol Brunson Phillips, and Carol Lou Young-Holt, for their contributions to this document; Karla Nygaard for editorial assistance; and Robert Cervantes, Kay Witcher, Janet Poole, Virginia Benson, Helen Nguyen, and Mary Smithberger, Child Development Division, California Department of Education, for review and recommendations on content. Thanks are also extended to the members of the national and California review panels and the Advisory Panel for Culturally Sensitive Care for their comments and suggestions.

The national panel members were T. Berry Brazelton, Laura Dittman, Richard Fiene, Magda Gerber, Asa Hilliard, Alice Honig, Jeree Pawl, Sally Provence, Eleanor Szanton, Yolanda Torres, Bernice Weissbourd, and Donna Wittmer. The California panel members were Dorlene Clayton, Dee Cuney, Ronda Garcia, Jacquelyne Jackson, Lee McKay, Janet Nielsen, Pearlene Reese, Maria Ruiz, June Sale, Patty Siegel, and Lenore Thompson. The members of the culturally sensitive care panel were Ruby Burgess, Jesus Cortez, Louise Derman-Sparks, Ron Henderson, Frances E. Kendall, Christina Guzman-Pederson, Carol Brunson Phillips, and Yolanda Torres.

About the Authors

Jesus Cortez is Director of the Center for Bilingual/Multicultural Studies in the College of Communication and Education at California State University, Chico, which offers credentials at the elementary, secondary, and graduate levels. An acknowledged expert in the fields of literacy and multiculturalism, Dr. Cortez is a consultant to educational institutions throughout the United States, Europe, and the Pacific Rim. He has also served on various state and national panels dealing with issues of literacy and bilingual/multicultural education.

Carol Brunson Phillips is a native of Chicago. She holds a B.A. in psychology from the University of Wisconsin, an M.A. in early childhood education from Erikson Institute, and a Ph.D. in education from Claremont Graduate School.

Throughout her career in early childhood education, Dr. Phillips has been involved in both teaching young children and training teachers, at first as a Head Start teacher and Instructor of Child Development at Prairie State College in Illinois. For 13 years she was a member of the Human Development Faculty at Pacific Oaks College in Pasadena, specializing in early childhood education and cultural influences on development. Currently, Dr. Phillips is Executive Director of the Council for Early Childhood Professional Recognition, Child Development Associate National Credentialing Program, in Washington, D.C.

Dr. Phillips has been the recipient of two outstanding fellowship awards: the first in 1980 from the Ford Foundation and the National Research Council, and the second in 1981 when she was named a Mina Shaughnessy Scholar by the U. S. Department of Education's Fund for the Improvement of Post-Secondary Education.

Janet Gonzalez-Mena, M.A., is an Instructor of Early Childhood Education at Napa Valley College. She was formerly Director of Child Care Services for Family Service Agency in San Mateo County. The agency's services included an infant/toddler center, a network of family child care homes, and a program of therapeutic child care for abused and neglected infants, toddlers, and preschoolers.

Ms. Gonzalez-Mena is a coauthor of *Infants, Toddlers, and Caregivers* and the author of *Infant/Toddler Caregiving: A Guide to Routines* and *English Experiences,* a program of English as a second language for preschool and kindergarten. She has also written articles about infants and toddlers and English as a second language for young children and one article on parent education for *Exchange*. With her husband, Frank Gonzalez-Mena, she coauthored *Experiences en Espanol*, a Spanish-language development program. She lives in a multiethnic, multiracial family.

Jayanthi Mistry, Ph.D., is Associate Professor at the Child Study Center, Tufts University. Dr. Mistry was formerly a researcher at the Center for the Development of Early

Education, Kamehameha Schools, in Honolulu. She conducted research on the sociocultural context of children's development and on the application of the research to planning educational programs for children (birth to five years of age) from multicultural backgrounds. She was also on the faculty of an experimental preservice training program that prepares elementary school teachers to work with children from multicultural backgrounds. Her publications, research, and teaching reflect the perspective that cognitive and social skills develop in the context of the young child's family and sociocultural environment through interaction with more experienced people. With Barbara Rogoff, Artin Göncü, and Christine Mosier, Dr. Mistry completed a study of the socialization of toddlers during routine daily activities in four cultural communities. In 1993 this research was published in the monograph *Guided Participation in Cultural Activity by Toddlers and Caregivers.*

Alicia F. Lieberman is a native of Paraguay. She holds a B.A. degree from the Hebrew University of Jerusalem, Israel, and a Ph.D. in psychology from Johns Hopkins University in Baltimore. Currently, she is Associate Professor in the Department of Psychiatry, University of California, San Francisco; and Senior Psychologist, Infant-Parent Program, San Francisco General Hospital. She is a board member of the National Center for Clinical Infant Programs in Washington, D.C.

Dr. Lieberman has specialized in the mental health needs of infants and their families. Her professional activities involve clinical work, teaching, consultation, and research in that area. A focus of her interest is the cultural diversity of child-rearing practices, values, and attitudes. She has recently completed an interventions research project in which she studied the patterns of infant-mother attachment in a sample of Latino mothers and infants. She has written and lectured on the topic of cultural sensitivity in intervention with ethnically diverse families.

Louise Derman-Sparks has worked for 25 years on issues of diversity and social justice as a preschool teacher, child care center director, parent, college teacher, researcher, and activist. A native of New York City, she holds a B.A. degree with a major in English and a minor in history from Brooklyn College and an M.A. in early and elementary education from the University of Michigan.

Ms. Derman-Sparks began her teaching career with the Ypsilanti Perry Preschool Project, then worked as a teacher supervisor with the Piagetian-based Early Childhood Program. For 15 years she has been a member of the human development faculty of Pacific Oaks College in Pasadena, where she teaches early childhood and parent education, an anti-bias curriculum, and the social-political contexts of human development.

The senior author of *Anti-Bias Curriculum: Tools for Empowering Young Children,* Ms. Derman-Sparks conducts in-service training and workshops for early childhood educators across the country. She is the recipient of several research grants to support her work on anti-bias education and is currently developing a manual of teacher-training materials intended to help early childhood teachers integrate an anti-bias curriculum into their programs.

Introduction

Families and communities are the ground-level generators and preservers of values and ethical systems. Individuals acquire a sense of self not only from observation of their own bodies and knowledge of their own thoughts but from their continuous relationship to others, especially close familial or community relations, and from the culture of their native place, the things, the customs, the honored deeds of their elders.

—John W. Gardner, "Community"

"Culture . . . is that complex whole which includes knowledge, belief, art, morals, law, custom, and any other capabilities and habits acquired by man as a member of society" (Tylor 1871, 1). Through culture children gain a sense of identity, a feeling of belonging, and beliefs about what is important in life, what is right and wrong, how to care for themselves and others, and what to celebrate, eat, and wear. When children are raised only in their home culture, they learn those lessons almost effortlessly. When they spend some of their formative years in child care with people who were not raised in their culture and who do not necessarily share the same family and community values, the learning of those important early lessons becomes more complex. That is the condition that many young children are now experiencing in the United States. By the year 2000 cultural diversity in child care will be the norm.

Because child care is becoming more culturally heterogeneous, caregivers can no longer be expected "naturally" to provide care that is consistent with paren-

tal care. Child care programs are experiencing an unparalleled growth in linguistic and cultural representation among the families and children served; therefore, understanding the impact of the out-of-home child care experience and the child's home culture on a child's development is crucial. The Program for Infant/Toddler Caregivers is particularly concerned about the impact of the situation

on children under three years of age. Research and practice have shown that for infants and toddlers to prosper in child care, their experiences should reflect a sensitivity by the caregiver to the home culture. When out-of-home caregivers support the child's primary language and culture, they not only help the child develop but also open the child care program's doors to the child's parents and community. Early caregiving in a child's native language and within familiar cultural rules makes child care a secure and supportive experience for the child. Culturally sensitive care influences positively the development of self-esteem, social competence, language, and intellectual competence.

This guide is written to assist infant/toddler caregivers in becoming more culturally sensitive. It is intended to help caregivers (1) better understand themselves and how they are influenced by their own cultural beliefs; (2) better understand the children and families they serve; and (3) learn a process of relating to cultural issues that will help them become more effective caregivers. The entire guide is based on three unifying themes that are sounded throughout the text:

- Cultural diversity is good and enriching for everyone.
- Cultural sensitivity is an ongoing process that continues to develop over time.
- Support of a child's full participation in his or her home culture is vital to optimal development.

The guide is divided into four sections, including a suggested resources section. Seven articles written by experts in infant/toddler development, multicultural education, and cultural sensitivity underscore the need for cultural sensitivity in infant/toddler care. The contributing authors present information, strategies, and insights for caregivers working with infants and toddlers from culturally diverse communities. The authors share the belief that commonalities and differences are fundamental to all humanity and that cultural diversity brings a rich mosaic to life. The purpose of the guide is to help readers analyze their own culturally driven behaviors, expand their ability to accept children and adults as they are, and be more appropriate in their response to people from different cultures.

The first article, "Culture: A Process That Empowers," by Carol Brunson Phillips, provides an ethnographic and historical perspective on culture and the care of young children. The author identifies basic characteristics of culture and discusses the differing and sometimes conflicting norms found in multicultural child care settings. The article closes with a discussion of what effect the empowering role of culture has on early development and what caregivers can do to support empowerment through cultural experience.

The second article, "Cultural Sensitivity in Routine Caregiving Tasks," by Janet Gonzalez-Mena, examines the importance of ongoing and open communication between parents and child care providers. The author focuses on the caregiving routines of feeding, diapering/toileting, and napping to exemplify how established practices may come into conflict with the culturally based approaches of parents. An open attitude of respect is recommended in communicating with parents about routines in the child care program. Through understanding the cultural reasons behind caregiving practices and preferences, caregivers may find acceptable ways to accommodate parents' requests.

In the third article, "Culture and Learning in Infancy," Jayanthi Mistry gives insight into how culture influences the learning experiences of children. She focuses on the style of interactions between adults and children who are members of the same cultural group. An appreciation of the differences in children's learning experiences will enable caregivers to be responsive to the interests and learning styles of children from culturally diverse backgrounds.

The fourth article, "Concerns of Immigrant Families," by Alicia F. Lieberman, deals with issues of stress and alienation that result when families are faced with immigration to a new country and possibly conflicting societal expectations in out-of-home child care. The importance of the relationship between parents and child care providers who differ culturally is underscored in this article, which also offers guidelines for dealing with recently arrived immigrant families.

The third section of the guide was written by Louise Derman-Sparks, who takes the reader on an adventure of self-evaluation, challenge, and professional cultural growth. Her three articles are relevant to the field of cultural awareness and sensitivity. Although it is not necessary to know everything there is to know about the cultures of the children with whom caregivers work, the process of *acknowledge, ask,* and *adapt* challenges even the most experienced caregiver to grow culturally. Through a process of thinking, writing, and evaluating, the reader learns concrete methods by which to identify, communicate, negotiate, and resolve issues of responsive caregiving.

References

Gardner, John W. 1991. "Community." Stanford, Calif.: Stanford University.

Taylor, Edward B. 1871. *Primitive Culture: Researches into the Development of Mythology, Philosophy, Religion, Art, and Custom.* Vol. 1. London: John Murray.

Section One:

The Importance of Culture in Early Development

Culture: A Process That Empowers

Carol Brunson Phillips

A major task of every society is to prepare its children to take their place in the world as adults. During a child's earliest years, the child's family is primarily responsible for seeing that preparation for adulthood takes place. Yet in today's complex world, the early years are not left solely to the family. As children enter child care at younger and younger ages, caregivers, especially those of infants and toddlers, share with parents the responsibilities of transmitting culture. What children learn from parents and caregivers is an *idea system* that goes deep into the values of a group of people. The learning goes far beyond the things one generally

associates with culture, such as art, music, or styles of dress. When children have acquired the culture of their society, they have learned to behave in socially expected ways and can, as adults, carry on the functions of the society as a whole.

The process by which families and caregivers teach children about culture is called *acculturation*. Acculturation includes all those aspects of child rearing that enable the child to know and understand a society's values, attitudes, beliefs, and behaviors. Participation in that process gives the child a special power to influence his or her environment in particular ways and to have a special impact on the world. For example, babies are born with the capability to make sounds; but many of those sounds are meaningless until they are shaped and organized into the words and sentences that the babies' families use. Thus, as children come to know the *ideas* that govern speech and language in their community, they gain the *power* to communicate. Their acculturation gives them that power. Acculturation plays an integral part in the creation of children's developmental competence. However, when the caregivers and families who are involved in this joint process are from different cultures, problems often arise that may negatively influence a child's development.

Cultural Appreciation and Enrichment

By studying how ideas about culture are presented in educational and child care settings, one can see why problems arise. Generally, information about cultural background and cultural influence is limited to the superficial aspects of culture. Educators and trainers traditionally treat culture with an almost exclusive emphasis on the celebrations, styles of dress, art, music, and food habits of different cultures. That emphasis creates a limited view of what *about* culture is important to development. Seldom is there an exploration of the deep structure of culture, of the idea system at work in the process of development.

The surface features of culture tend to be presented in educational and child care settings in one of two ways: (1) by teaching *cultural appreciation,* the "let's learn about people from other cultures because they are human just like us" approach; or (2) by providing *cultural enrichment,* the "let me show you why you should be proud of who you are" approach. Therefore, when educators and caregivers deal with culture, the approach tends to be characterized by the following features:

1. The approach is a "tourist" one, emphasizing the exotic elements of groups, such as the holidays and costumes. The teacher or caregiver views the children in the same way a tour guide treats visitors to a strange place: they "visit" non-White cultures, then "go home to the daily classroom, which reflects only the dominant culture" (Derman-Sparks 1989, 7).

2. The approach has an international flavor favoring the traditions of a group in its ethnic homeland outside the United States. Teachers or caregivers often choose to highlight those aspects, even when the same ethnic group has a different lifestyle in this country.

3. The selection of which culture to learn about is often arbitrary, bearing no relation to the background or culture of the children in the classroom. The teacher or caregiver chooses her or his favorite group, usually the one with the most exciting and colorful customs.

4. The focus is on the historical achievements of the group or on the romanticized past and highlights the superstar members of the group. The teacher or caregiver may fail to see cultural meaning in contemporary events and in the more mundane, everyday lifestyles of a group.

Surrounding children with artifacts and customs that are a part of their history, homes, and communities is important (Hankerson 1987). However, when that approach becomes the sole emphasis in multicultural curriculum efforts, it diverts attention from the more fundamental role that culture plays in the development of children's social, emotional, physical, and intellectual well-being. The challenge for caregivers and trainers of caregivers is to develop strategies to help in understanding the critical importance of culture to human development and to strive to move beyond cultural appreciation and enrichment to cultural empowerment.

Cultural Empowerment

Although the view that culture empowers people to function is relatively new to the field of early childhood education and care, it is emerging as a most

3

appropriate base for developing cultural sensitivity. Unlike the goals of cultural appreciation and cultural enrichment, the goal of cultural empowerment is not to teach culture to children but to teach children in a culturally consistent context. Caregivers must become aware that they probably will never learn a cultural curriculum that they will teach; instead, they will learn ways to relate to issues of culture. It will take work and study to understand the subtleties of how culture influences and empowers people. Such an endeavor is especially important for those caregivers responsible for the care of children who come from cultures that are different from their own.

The cultural empowerment approach helps the caregiver provide culturally consistent settings for children—settings built on the attitudes, values, and behavioral expectations of the home culture of the child. The knowledge caregivers need to create such settings resides in understanding the deep struc-

ture of culture and the process whereby culture works to support development.

Children build their basic senses of trust, security, and stability on cultural foundations learned at home. Therefore, continuity, consistency, and respect in the caregiving environment for cultural foundations are essential to children's continuing growth. When the family's culture is ignored or when caregivers react to culturally different children as though they are deficient, underdeveloped, or incompetent, children experience problems in communication, in getting their needs met, and in establishing relationships. Under those conditions children lose their power to develop their overall well-being.

The cultural empowerment of children involves eliminating caregivers' ignorance of and negative reactions to cultural differences. One way to begin to do so is for caregivers to learn more about how culture is and is not transmitted. The following important concepts about the process of acculturation are discussed in this article:

1. Culture is learned.
2. Culture is characteristic of groups.
3. Culture is a set of rules for behavior.
4. Individuals are embedded to different degrees within a culture.
5. Cultures borrow and share rules.
6. Members of a cultural group may be proficient in cultural behavior but unable to describe the rules.

Awareness and understanding of these concepts will help in building relationships with families, a necessary part of providing culturally consistent and empowering care for infants and toddlers.

Culture Is Learned

No one is born acculturated; instead, everyone is born with a biological capability to learn. *What* each person learns depends on the cultural rules of the people who raise him or her. Some rules are taught with words; for example, "hold your fork in your right hand and your knife in your left." Other rules are demonstrated by actions; for example, when to smile or how close to stand when talking to someone.

Because culture is learned, it is a mistake to assume a person's culture by how he or she looks. Someone can be ethnically Black and culturally Irish. A person can also become bicultural or tricultural by experiencing and learning the rules of other cultures.

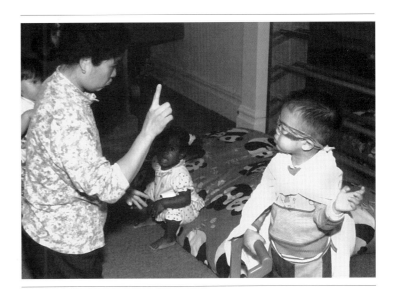

Culture Is Characteristic of Groups

The rules and beliefs of a culture are shared by the group, not invented by the individual; the rules of the *group* that are passed from one generation to the next form the core of the culture. It is a mistake to confuse individual differences with group differences. Within a culture each person develops a unique personality as a result of his or her personal history and some behavioral characteristics that are shared with other members of the group.

Culture Is a Set of Rules for Behavior

You cannot "see" culture because you cannot see the rules. You can see only the products of culture in the sense that you can see the behaviors the rules produce. Yet cultural rules do not *cause* behavior; they *influence* people to behave similarly in ways that help them understand each other.

By understanding your culture's rules, you know how to greet a person younger than you or older than you, a friend, or a stranger. Cultural rules shape food preferences, lifestyle, and celebrations, determining, for example, whether you celebrate the sun or the moon or whether you wear a dress or pants or nothing at all. The rules give meaning to all the events and experiences of life. The essence of culture is in the rules that produce the behaviors, not the behaviors themselves.

Individuals Are Embedded to Different Degrees Within a Culture

Because culture is learned, it can be learned well by some people in the group and learned less well by others. While children are growing up, they usually learn the core rules of their culture; yet they may not always learn every cultural rule equally well. Some families are more tradition oriented, others less so. Even when families and individuals learn the cultural rules, they may not always behave according to what they have learned. Some people are conformists; others are nonconformists. As a consequence of both phenomena, the behavior of members of a culture will vary, depending on how deeply embedded their experiences are within the core of a culture. When you work as a caregiver with individual families, thinking about behavioral variations in this way will help you understand why, for example, all Japanese do not always act as Japanese.

Cultures Borrow and Share Rules

Every cultural group has its own set of core behavioral rules and is, therefore, unique. However, some of the rules of culture A may be the same as the rules of culture B. That situation happens because cultural rules evolve and change over time. Sometimes, when two groups

have extensive contact with one another, they influence each other in some areas. Thus, two groups of people may speak the same language but have different rules about roles for women. If you understand that possibility, you will not be confused when a person from another culture is so much like you in some ways but is so different in others.

Members of a Cultural Group May Be Proficient in Cultural Behavior but Unable to Describe the Rules

Acculturation is a natural process that begins at birth. During the process individuals are not conscious that their ideas and behavior are being shaped by a unique set of rules. A four-year-old who is proficient in language could not, if asked, diagram a sentence or explain the rules of grammar. In the same way people become thoroughly proficient in cultural behavior without consciously knowing that they are behaving according to rules. This natural process explains why you cannot walk up to people and ask them to teach you their culture. Nor, probably, could you explain your own.

Practical Suggestions for Becoming Culturally Sensitive

1. *Make a commitment to learn about the cultural expectations of the families whose children are in your care and eliminate any stereotyped and biased attitudes you may have toward cultures different from your own.*

   There are no shortcuts to achieving this goal; it is a continuous process. A conscious choice is required to create a climate in which dialogue about culture occurs on a regular basis; caregivers and parents can raise issues openly; and decisions about what is best for children are collaborative, resulting from a negotiated consensus. Where to begin is not difficult—begin at the beginning. *Commit yourself to identifying and eliminating your own cultural biases.* Remember that everyone has biases from growing up and living in a society in which negative attitudes and practices are institutionalized in the political, social, and economic systems that govern one's everyday life. Biases in institutional systems give privilege to one group over others by declaring the characteristics of that group superior to all others. Because the biases sometimes take the form of racist, classist, and sexist ideas, you must deal with those also.

There are many written resources to help you explore your biases (see Katz 1978; Ryan 1976). One organization that specializes in such resources is Educational Equity Concepts in New York City.

2. *Actively search for subtle messages of bias in your daily life.*

One beginning exercise to become aware of how biased messages subtly penetrate your life involves examining the ways in which different people and their behavior are represented on prime-time television. Arrange with a group of caregivers, or with both caregivers and parents, to watch a series of the same television programs; then meet for a follow-up discussion of what you saw and did not see on the television screen. You will probably find that the characters represent a limited range; for example, the hustling, street-smart Puerto Rican, the dumb Mexican, the mobster Italian, the violent Black, the quiet and submissive Native American. No matter how much you may want to deny that those images affect your attitude about various groups of people, they do. An important step in the exercise is to look for appropriate models in the community to counteract the negative mass-media stereotypes. This kind of exercise can help eliminate your own bias if done sensi-

tively. Once bias is acknowledged, it is necessary to go beyond the negative images to the positive ones you want to share with the children in your care.

3. *Find out accurate information about the culture of the children in your care and determine how to use the information in your caregiving setting.*

Keep in mind the six concepts of acculturation presented earlier. Avoid focusing only on artifacts. Instead, try to get at attitudes and values in the deep structure of culture, knowing that various families are embedded to different degrees in their culture and that people's cultural rules will not be on the tips of their tongues. Talk with families about what they do at home that they feel is particularly culturally significant, what values they have about the right and wrong ways to discipline children, and what ways they want their children to express anger or relate to authority figures. Ask how they feel children should act toward their friends and toward their siblings. Have them describe their style of bathing their babies, feeding them, and playing with them. Remember that you, too, operate on cultural rules and should share them in the discussions.

4. *Read about other cultures and discuss what you read with your families and colleagues.*

   Ask people from other cultures whether the information you read is of value and discuss with them when and how to apply it. A good deal of theoretical as well as practical material appears in the early childhood education literature. The most visible and well-known body of information in recent years has resulted from the multicultural education movement that began in earnest in the 1960s (*Teaching* 1977). The movement has had an enormous impact and has generated a large body of curriculum material. (See Kendall 1983 for resources listed in the appendixes.) Note that much of what has been written contains stereo-

types and biases. Be cautious and remain open to other people's opinions about what you read.

5. *Help families deal with issues of cultural conflict.*

   Children and families experience conflict when society devalues them by demanding that they give up their culture to achieve success (Hale-Benson 1986; *Extracting* 1986). Often, families do not realize that young children can become bicultural. Family members think they must choose between their culture and the dominant one. Sometimes they feel that the dominant culture is more important because they want their children to be successful in the broader society. That conflict can be resolved through open discussions and program approaches that support families in maintaining their cultural integrity while they are acquiring skills to function in the larger society.

6. *Work consciously to establish a program approach that both helps children function in their own cultural community and builds their competence in the culture of the larger society.*

   Set up caregiving settings that emphasize the following strategies:

   a. Use culturally appropriate (culturally empowering) child-rearing strategies in the daily functions of the caregiving environment.

   b. Use children's native language as an appropriate bridge to communicating with children and their families.

   c. Select and train program staff who understand how culture influences their own behavior and who are proficient in the culture of the children.

d. Establish agreed-on strategies to foster development in the children's own culture. (For example, develop both English and the native language through the natural use of both in child care, whenever possible.)

e. Establish agreed-on strategies to facilitate the development in children of skills necessary for successful functioning in the dominant culture. (This way of helping children is most effectively done by programs adopting an additive approach to care that helps children gain additional skills rather than substitute dominant-culture skills for home-culture skills.)

To grow and thrive, children need cultural skills—skills that will provide them with power and productivity in mainstream North America and with a sense of meaning in life, history, and home. With your help they will learn those skills and form their views about who they are and their visions about who they can be. Children can see themselves only as they are seen by the adults in their lives. When children see themselves through your culturally sensitive eyes, they will see their power.

References

Alike and Different: Exploring Our Humanity with Young Children (Revised edition). 1992. Edited by Bonnie Neugebauer. Washington, D.C.: National Association for the Education of Young Children.

Derman-Sparks, Louise, and the A.B.C. Task Force. 1989. *Anti-Bias Curriculum: Tools for Empowering Young Children.* Washington, D.C.: National Association for the Education of Young Children.

Extracting Learning Styles from Social/ Cultural Diversity: Studies of Five American Minorities. 1986. Edited by Lee Morris. Norman, Okla.: Southwest Teacher Corps Network.

Hale-Benson, Janice. 1986. *Black Children: Their Roots, Culture, and Learning Styles.* Baltimore: Johns Hopkins University Press.

Hankerson, Henry. 1987. "Quality Programs for Infants and Toddlers: Focusing on Multicultural Education," in *Multicultural Learning in Early Childhood Education.* Edited by Kevin J. Swick. Little Rock, Ark.: Southern Association on Children Under Six.

Katz, Judith. 1978. *White Awareness: A Handbook for Anti-Racism Training.* Norman: University of Oklahoma Press.

Kendall, Frances E. 1983. *Diversity in the Classroom: A Multicultural Approach to the Education of Young Children.* New York: Teachers College Press, Teachers College, Columbia University.

Phillips, Carol Brunson. 1988. "Nurturing Diversity for Today's Children and Tomorrow's Leaders," *Young Children,* Vol. 43 (January), 42–47.

Ryan, William. 1976. *Blaming the Victim.* New York: Random House, Inc.

Teaching in a Multicultural Society. 1977. Edited by Dolores E. Cross, Gwendolyn C. Baker, and Lindley J. Stiles. New York: Free Press.

Section Two:
Multicultural Issues in Child Care

Cultural Sensitivity in Routine Caregiving Tasks

Janet Gonzalez-Mena

Every day you bring your personal values and beliefs to your work with children and families. Therefore, it is essential to understand how your caregiving practices reflect and represent the culture in which you were raised. As explained by Carol Brunson Phillips in the previous article, the culture you come from has taught you particular beliefs, values, rules, and expectations for behavior. And the way you learned those lessons, particularly in infancy, was through early interactions with your family members and caregivers, involving such basic activities as feeding, toileting, and napping. One reason caregivers have a profound effect on the

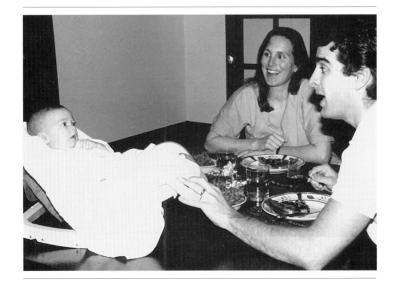

development of infants and toddlers is that caregivers engage in those everyday caregiving activities many times a day. While doing those routine tasks, caregivers pass on important cultural messages about how life should be lived. It is vital to understand that when you are caring for infants and toddlers, you are participating in a subtle form of teaching.

Equally important is understanding that the personal and cultural values reflected in the child-rearing practices of the parents of the infants and toddlers in your care may not agree with yours and that you may not be aware of parents' values when they ask you to do a routine in a particular way. For example, parents who endorse caregiving practices that stress self-help skills and competence building in infants, such as feeding oneself and putting oneself to sleep, usually want their children to grow up to be self-sufficient. The goal behind those practices often is to produce an independent, unique individual. In contrast to that goal, a child's sense of belonging to a group may be a more important issue than a separate identity for parents who see optimum functioning in the group or family system as the most important priority. These parents may expect adults and older children to help a child with eating throughout early childhood and consider falling asleep to be something the child always does in the presence of others. Parents who endorse those practices tend to value the goal of interdependence more than one of independence.

Both of those goals are valid. Yet the difference between them is fundamental, and valuing one or the other for personal or cultural reasons influences the way caregiving practices are handled. Knowing that different values are reflected in how routine caregiving practices are carried out will allow you to acknowledge, work with, and resolve conflicts that invariably arise when people hold different viewpoints. Only then can you truly provide infants and toddlers with the sensitive care that supports their development within their family and cultural context.

This article deals with some of the cultural differences reflected in child-rearing practices associated with three basic caregiving routines: toilet training, feeding, and sleeping/napping. You will probably not be familiar with some of the cultural positions people hold about the three routines. You may not even be aware of your own values connected with them until you find yourself in a conflict with a parent or a fellow caregiver.

Consider these three situations and think about your probable response:

1. *Toilet training.* A new parent explains to you that her one-year-old child is toilet trained and insists that you leave off the diapers.

2. *Feeding.* The mother of a toddler is upset by the mess she sees when she discovers that you are letting him feed himself. She asks you to spoon-feed her child as she does at home, "so he eats more, doesn't get so messy, and less food is wasted."

3. *Napping.* Another parent explains that his baby is used to falling asleep in

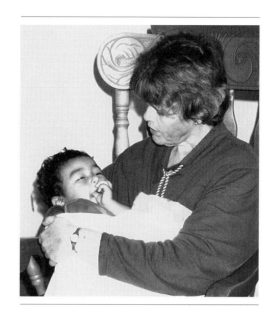

someone's arms, not by herself in a crib in a separate room. He asks that you hold the child until she goes to sleep each day.

Now reflect on your process. When you considered the three scenarios, was your natural inclination to think about such things as your program policies, philosophy and guidelines, developmental theory, research studies, or even licensing regulations? If so, you acted as most caregivers would. Caregivers often raise such issues in responding to a parent who asks for something to be done differently from that of the child care program's standard routine, especially when the request is for something that seems unreasonable and difficult to carry out.

Child care programs in family homes and centers are serving an increasingly diverse population. Parents may or may not have chosen your program because of its philosophy and caregiving practices. It is vital that you find out how the parents view their child's care. Observe. Ask. Good communication with parents is the key to providing the best care for each infant or toddler. Communication is especially important in a culturally diverse program. This article examines three caregiving routines.

Toilet Training

Most experts (e.g., Leach, Spock, and Brazelton) agree that to start toilet training much before two years of age is unwise. In their view the child's readiness is the main factor in deciding when to start toilet training. This readiness involves the child's physical, intellectual, and emotional abilities to control, understand, and cooperate in the toilet-training process. The goal of toilet training in the experts' approach is to get children to handle their own toileting without adult help. For that reason the children must be mature enough to walk, talk, handle clothing, and so forth. Toilet training is considered an important step in the child's growing independence.

As sensible as the experts' approach to toilet training may appear, there are other points of view on the matter. For some parents the goal of toilet training is to create a partnership between parent and child; these parents may also want to eliminate the use of diapers as early as possible. Eventually, the self-help skills and independence in toileting will come, but that development is not seen as necessary or important to begin the toilet-training process.

Janice Hale talks about an approach to toilet training that is different from the experts' wait-until-after-two-years-of-age approach. Hale states that in some cultures babies are held so much of the time that caregivers can give "an immediate response to urination and bowel movements. Hence, from an early age, there is an association in the infant's mind between these functions and action from the mother. Consequently, when the

mother seeks to toilet train the child, . . . the child is accustomed to her direct involvement in this process" (Hale 1983, 70).

The transition from wearing diapers to using the toilet is more startling for infants whose bodily functions typically occur when they are physically separate from the mother. The mother begins to become actively involved in the child's bowel and bladder activities after many months of giving them only cursory attention. A toilet-training process based on readiness, beginning suddenly when the caregiver perceives that the child is ready for it, is very different from an ongoing training process based on a partnership between a caregiver and child who

maintain close physical contact with one another.

If a mother is sensitive to her one-year-old's signals and manages the child's toileting without diapers, it is quite reasonable for her to ask the child's caregiver to do the same. Her expectations are that the caregiver will form the same kind of partnership that she and her infant have developed together. Therefore, when she talks about the child being toilet trained, she does not mean that the child will go to the bathroom and use the toilet independently. She means that the caregiver will be able to read the child's signals and take the child to the toilet.

Caregivers who have experience with children from a variety of backgrounds know that many young babies often do not have wet diapers. That observation supports the idea that an early adult-child partnership and early toilet training are possible. Whether or not you advocate a particular toilet-training practice, you need to know that variations in children's responses to toilet training may reflect a cultural rather than a physical difference. The infant's capability for early toilet training comes from continual physical contact with the caregiver and the caregiver's belief that dry diapers are possible, even for babies.

Communicating About Toilet Training

Understanding that a parent may have a different view of toilet training because of cultural beliefs and practices is crucial when communicating about different approaches. In the following scenario, notice the miscommunication that occurs:

The mother arrives to pick up her twelve-month-old son and finds him playing on the floor in wet diapers while the caregiver is busy fixing the afternoon snack. Frowning as she carries him over to the diapering table, the mother quickly changes her son. Her displeasure shows on her face throughout the process, but she does not say anything until she is on her way out the door. Then, as a parting remark, the mother says over her shoulder to the caregiver, "I wish you'd be more alert and catch my son before he wets! At home he's toilet trained."

"Sure he's trained!" the caregiver says sarcastically under her breath, as though she does not believe it. Then she adds, loud enough for the mother to hear, "He's not trained. You are!"

The parent and the caregiver have a problem. Obviously, there has been no prior communication about the parent's expectations about toilet training, dry diapers, and the like. The caregiver has not talked with the parent about the child care program's expectations or about what is reasonable for a parent to expect when his or her child is being cared for in a group setting. Another problem is the attitude of nonacceptance expressed by both the caregiver and the parent about each other's caregiving practices.

If you were in the caregiver's shoes, you might have difficulty following that parent's practice, even if you wanted to. You might feel you could not possibly be holding one baby all the time in order to learn the subtle body signals the baby sends just before he or she wets. How could you possibly take care of more than one infant and hold each all the time? But if you understand the mother's experience, her point of view, and her definition of toilet training, your attitude toward her will be different from just thinking of her as lacking in knowledge.

The parent, too, might have a more accepting attitude of you and your caregiving practices if you had had a conversation with her about the difference between caring for infants and toddlers in groups and caring for one baby alone at home. That conversation between the parent and caregiver needs to begin *before* the child is in care, during a parent-caregiver orientation. The discussion between parents and caregivers is a two-way street. In addition to sharing information, the mother and caregiver need to engage in some problem solving about consistency of care and shared expectations for the child's care.

Feeding Practices

Self-feeding of infants and toddlers is a messy but an important step toward independence. According to the experts (e.g., Leach and Spock), it is important to encourage babies to take part in the feeding process, even though a mess results. Leach even suggests that babies be allowed to play around in their food to get the full benefit of the sensory experience. Almost everyone who has been involved

in infant/toddler child care has been confronted with a parent unhappy about a mess. Indeed, some caregivers may also be uncomfortable with a mess.

There may be a number of reasons why some parents or some caregivers object to allowing babies to feed themselves, even when they are capable of doing so. In some cultures food is revered and is never considered a plaything, either at the table or as an activity, such as finger painting with pudding. Parents or caregivers who have experienced severe food shortages or who empathize with the circumstances of starvation will be horrified at the thought of playing with food.

When there is a core belief about the importance of cleanliness, experiencing the tactile properties of food and playing with it are discouraged. Parents who have little time to feed their babies or clean them afterwards may find that spoon-feeding them until they can eat neatly and efficiently by themselves is more expedient, even though some children may reach that point as late as four years of age. Telling parents about the importance of taking time to feed their children is easy enough, but many will not hear the message because they have a different set of priorities and values. However, in the child care setting there is time for children to learn self-feeding skills and for adults to clean up the mess. Again, it is important to recognize that values and beliefs are what drive your caregiving practices and that you need to discuss feeding practices in your parent-caregiver orientation and ongoing conversations.

Aimee Emiko Sodetani-Shibata (1981, p. 98) makes the following point about a different approach to self-feeding in her culture: "Children are fed until they acquire the ability to handle a spoon on their own—but parents often resort to the use of both self-feeding and adult-feeding. . . . As the child approaches school-age, feeding by the parents is weaned, and it is stopped when the child enters school. . . . Orderliness and tidiness are highly stressed."

The issue may be different from one of cleanliness or the value of food. The issue may be about early independence. Teaching self-help skills is not a universal value in all cultures. On the contrary, in writing about her culture, Consuelo Aquino (1981, p. 176) states: "The baby is considered a very precious thing. As the baby grows, he is watched closely with loving concern. Expectations are kept below the child's potential, [and] all problems are met indirectly by distracting and pacifying the child. This leisurely maturation process influences the mother's action in feeding. . . . Children tend to be dependent, but this is an accepted norm within the culture." Children from the culture Aquino describes would more likely be spoon-fed for a longer period than would children from cultures in which early independence is a priority. Babies in Aquino's culture also might not be expected to go to sleep without help.

Sleeping/Napping Routines

As in feeding and toileting routines, different cultural and personal values support different practices related to sleeping and napping. The idea that babies should sleep in separate cribs in a quiet room away from the family activity is not a universal belief. In many cultures people believe it is important for the infant and caregiver to maintain close physical proximity; and when the baby needs to sleep, he or she does so while being carried about. In some cultures, as Hale (1983, p. 25) states, "socialization

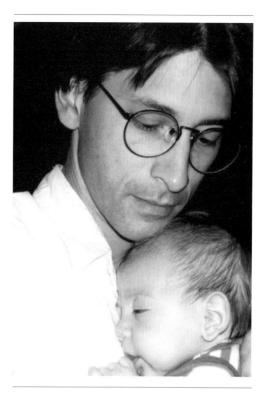

emphasizes the closeness of people. Physical and psychological closeness is reinforced by encouragement of body contact between people." When families immigrate to the United States, they bring the roots of their child-rearing practices from their homeland. Hale discusses the influences of the "old country" on sleeping arrangements. In countries in which children are typically breast-fed for a longer period than they are in the United States and held a great deal of the time, even when they are not being breast-fed, the children also usually sleep with their mothers. Not all families have space for members to sleep alone and in separate rooms. Whatever the reason, a mother who is used to having her baby sleeping with her may well request that the child not be put in a crib to learn to sleep alone.

Values about sleeping and napping routines often cause a conflict when the caregiving practices at home do not match those at the child care setting. In many programs in the United States, the policy of the child care program, the licensing requirements, or the interpretation of child care licensing regulations dictate separate sleeping arrangements for infants and toddlers. Consequently, when children come from home settings with different caregiving practices for sleeping, they experience a major inconsistency in care. The situation becomes difficult for all concerned—baby, caregiver, and parents—when babies are accustomed to being held and rocked to sleep at home but in the child care setting are placed alone in a crib in a quiet, separate sleeping room. No wonder the children have difficulty falling asleep when they first come into group care.

Again, it is important to be sensitive and responsive to the needs of individual parents and babies and to be realistic about what is possible and best for the child in the child care setting. Together you and the parents will need to explore how you can come to a mutually satisfying solution. With this particular issue you may have to include your licensing person in your discussions to be sure the requirements are truly appropriate to the infant's needs and consistent with the family's child-rearing practices and are not simply a culturally biased interpretation of the regulation.

Summary

There are no "right" answers about values or the extent to which caregivers should adapt their practices in any of the situations discussed in this chapter. Even practices that are considered developmentally appropriate in infant and toddler caregiving routines are influenced by cultural, professional, and personal beliefs. The practices reflect the dominant culture's beliefs and values. It is important for everyone in the child care field to be knowledgeable about both accepted caregiving practices and other child-rearing beliefs and practices, keeping in mind that in another cultural context that culture's practices would be held as the accepted practices for that setting.

Diversity of beliefs and values often brings conflict. In child care many diverse beliefs manifest themselves in different caregiving practices related to everyday, routine activities. The purpose of this guide is to help you tune in to the sensitivity required to work with someone else's baby. In this article various routines and associated values and caregiving practices have been brought to your attention to help sensitize you to the differences you will encounter regularly as a caregiver. Such differences are inevitable with the increasing cultural diversity that communities are experiencing today.

What is not necessarily inevitable is that one cultural view remains or becomes dominant over another. Instead of automatically responding in your usual ways, take time to listen to parents who want something different for their babies from what you ordinarily provide. Put

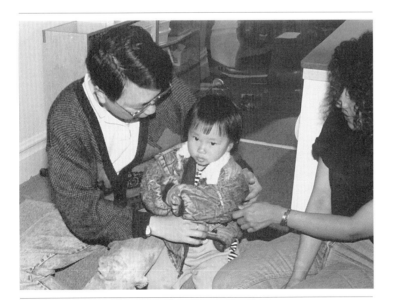

yourself in their shoes. Tune in. Be sensitive. Try to find out what is really behind the request. Have ongoing conversations with parents about child-rearing and family practices. Understanding parents' cultural backgrounds comes through finding out about the culture firsthand, not by labeling or stereotyping a family because it belongs to a particular group.

Be sensitive to the child's feelings. When infants and toddlers experience little continuity between home and child care, they will have a difficult time. It is important to build bridges. Provide consistency with the child rearing at home whenever possible so that the child will feel comfortable in care outside the home. A good idea is to talk with all the parents about routine caregiving and family practices as part of your enrollment and orientation procedures *before* you have the child in your care. By doing so, you will learn what the child is used to.

When you understand different values and beliefs, you will be able to collaborate with parents to develop culturally consistent care for infants and toddlers by supporting the culture of the home as much as possible. To give that kind of support, you need to find ways to adapt to parents' requests and babies' needs, even when they do not fit in exactly with your usual practices.

References

Aquino, Consuelo. 1981. "The Filipino in America," in *Culture and Childrearing*. Edited by Ann L. Clark. Philadelphia: F. A. Davis, Co.

Brazelton, T. Berry. 1962. "A Child Oriented Approach to Toilet Training," *Pediatrics*, Vol. 29 (January), 121–28.

Caudill, W., and H. Weinstein. 1969. "Maternal Care and Infant Behavior in Japan and America," *Psychiatry,* Vol. 32, 12–43.

Gonzalez-Mena, Janet, and Diane W. Eyer. 1992. *Infants, Toddlers, and Caregivers* (Third, revised edition). Mountain View, Calif.: Mayfield Publishing Co.

Hale, Janice. 1983. "Black Children: Their Roots, Culture, and Learning Styles," in *Understanding the Multicultural Experience in Early Childhood Education.* Edited by Olivia N. Saracho and Bernard Spodek. Washington, D.C.: National Association for the Education of Young Children.

Leach, Penelope. 1978. *Your Baby and Child: From Birth to Age Five.* New York: Alfred A. Knopf, Inc.

Morrow, Robert D. 1987. "Cultural Differences—Be Aware!" *Academic Therapy,* Vol. 23 (November), 143–49.

Resources for Infant Educarers Manual. 1989. Edited by Magda Gerber. Los Angeles: Resources for Infant Educarers.

Sandoval, Mercedes C., and Maria C. De La Roza. 1986. "Cross-Cultural Perspective for Serving the Hispanic Client," in *Cross-Cultural Training for Mental Health Professionals.* Edited by Harriet P. Lefley and Paul B. Pedersen. Springfield, Ill.: Charles C. Thomas, Pubs.

Sodetani-Shibata, Aimee Emiko. 1981. "The Japanese American," in *Culture and Childrearing.* Edited by Ann L. Clark. Philadelphia: F. A. Davis, Co.

Spock, Benjamin, and Michael B. Rothenberg. 1985. *Dr. Spock's Baby and Child Care.* New York: NAL/ Dutton.

Culture and Learning in Infancy

Jayanthi Mistry

Children in all cultural communities learn valued skills and behaviors through social interaction with parents and other primary caregivers. Many differences in the learning styles and learning skills of children, even those of infants, are directly related to the early lessons of their home culture. This article explores differences in the learning experiences of children from different home cultures and the ways in which caregivers can support children who are accustomed to learning in cultural settings that are different from the group care setting.

Culture and Learning

There are major differences in the degree to which various skills and behaviors are valued and, therefore, emphasized by different cultural communities. The differences are embedded in the people's way of life, beliefs about the world, and cultural goals. When caregivers observe children in their home culture, they can learn how the family views children's skills in achieving particular cultural goals. Cultural differences that influence early learning can be observed in the following situations:

- The ways in which parents handle routines and set up the environment
- The kinds of learning and skill-development activities available to children

- The manner in which children are exposed to language
- The style of interaction adults use with their infants and toddlers

Routines

The way parents arrange the daily routines and schedules at home conveys to children the appropriate behaviors, beliefs, and attitudes of the family and cultural community. For example, children learn to eat by using utensils, such as a spoon or chopsticks, or learn to eat with their hands, depending on the family's

culturally based mealtime routines and activities. Thus culture has a direct impact on the skills children learn from routines.

The schedule of the day, or the way time is structured, is also learned. Some cultural communities do not value or follow regular schedules (e.g., set eating and sleeping times) for their home routines. In those communities the children learn to be on the lookout for novelty and change. A baby who can adjust to continual changes in routines or situations is considered desirable. In other communities the baby's adaptation to a regular routine is encouraged. In such communities children learn to focus their attention on predictable patterns in the daily schedule.

The timing of toilet training is another example of the influence of culturally based routines on learning. As Janet Gonzalez-Mena describes in her article, some cultural communities handle toilet training as a partnership with the children when they are quite young. In those cultures children learn the routine through being cooperative. In contrast, children in the dominant U.S. culture are trained or taught to manage the toileting routine through independent action when they are physically mature and able to talk. In other words, the children learn through becoming increasingly independent.

Learning Activities

Beliefs about the ways children learn differ a great deal from culture to culture. The differences can be seen in how adults spend time with children. In some cultural communities children learn by simply being present as adults go about their jobs and household activities. Adults do not create learning situations to teach their children. Instead, children are responsible for learning culturally valued behaviors and practices by observing and

being around adults during the course of the day. In other cultural communities children are naturally included in adult jobs and activities. For example, a toddler may be cared for by a mother who runs the family store. In that setting the child is assured a role in the action, at least as a close observer. The child is responsible for learning through active observation and gradual participation.

Some cultural communities frequently keep children apart from the parents' work and recreational activities. In these cultures adults often provide children with a scaled-down version of adult activities, such as toy versions of equipment that adults use in their jobs. During parent-child interactions in the activities, the parents adjust their speech and actions to the child's level of skill and understanding. In those situations the adults may become overly preoccupied with adapting learning situations for children. The adults can easily lose sight of the active role children play in managing their own learning through observation of social activity apart from adult-directed teaching/learning situations.

Infants in some cultural communities have access to all aspects of their parents' activities and environment. In New Guinea, for example, infants have access to all the tools and equipment that their parents use and become so self-reliant that they handle knives and fire safely by the time they are able to walk (Sorenson 1979). However, they do not recklessly thrust themselves into unappreciated dangers. This example puts the emphasis on baby-proofing the environment in the United States in a different light. Baby-proofing is not necessarily a universally appropriate practice; it is related to whether adults take responsibility for adapting the environment for children or whether children take responsibility for learning what is safe and what is not.

Language Learning

The area of language learning provides another example of differences among cultures in approaches to learning. Some cultural communities emphasize adults having "conversations" with infants. In contrast, children in other cultural communities learn language primarily through eavesdropping and observing or through hours spent overhearing adults' conversations (Ward 1986; Heath 1983).

Differences in language learning appear early in infancy. In some cultures mothers carry on a "dialogue" even with a one-week-old infant. Adults endow the baby's smallest vocalizations with meaning and intentionality and react to them emotionally. In other cultural communities parents talk for, rather than to, the baby (Cole and Cole 1989).

Language learning practices with older infants also vary from culture to culture. The culturally based practice of repeating what a toddler has just said, with the goal of expanding his or her language, may seem odd to adults in many cultures. Similarly, many adults believe that asking toddlers to label pictures while a storybook is being read serves no useful purpose. An adult already knows the names of things, and it is considered inappropriate to seek from a child information that one already knows.

Verbal Versus Observational Learning

Various examples cited previously make reference to one of the major aspects of the learning process that varies among cultural communities; that is, an emphasis on direct, verbal learning in contrast to nonverbal, observational learning. Although experts in the child care field may consider an emphasis on verbal learning appropriate and desirable, that belief is not universal; it is culturally based. Because of the influence of culture, you need to recognize the cultural basis of your own assumptions about val-

ued skills and the nature of learning. For example, verbal expressiveness and a verbal means of learning may be valued because they are necessary skills in a literate society. Two-year-olds who are able to express themselves verbally may be considered advanced because they are thought to have a head start on the verbal skills that are valued for later schooling.

In addition to the importance of literacy and success in school, verbal skills may be valued for many other culturally based reasons. Those values can be seen in the behavior of parents and children in various cultural communities. Early on, babies in some cultures spend a fair amount of time by themselves—sleeping in separate rooms and amusing themselves in their playpens while parents do household chores and other activities. These children learn to depend on verbal communication to get the attention of adults; for example, by calling out to the parent or caregiver.

In contrast, babies in other cultural communities are often in physical contact with their caregiver. They sleep with their parents or are carried around constantly. These babies are likely to learn to depend on nonverbal communication, such as gestures with their hands or changes in posture or muscle tone, to get their needs met.

In some cultural communities parents value alert but calm and placid styles of interaction and temperament. These parents do not engage in the highly stimulating, playful, face-to-face interactions with their babies that U.S. experts consider valuable for learning. Infants accustomed to quiet social contact with adults may become overstimulated by the more intense and active styles of interaction that one sees in many child care programs. This difference between home care and group child care is often subtle but can cause trouble for infants and toddlers.

Caregiving in Different Learning Situations

Culture influences how caregivers arrange and set up activities for infants and toddlers, how caregivers help children in those activities, and how caregivers interact with children. Like parents, caregivers structure the environment and create schedules to teach attitudes and beliefs that they consider appropriate. For example, infant/toddler caregivers who believe it is important to foster social skills at an early age design their environments and activities in such a way that the children have many opportunities for social contact during all play and caregiving activities.

Caregivers also teach what they believe to be appropriate behavior when they provide guidance to children. Some use an approach to providing guidance that is mostly nonverbal. These caregivers may model or demonstrate a particular behavior as the child watches. In contrast, caregivers from other cultural backgrounds may be verbal and direct. They may tend to engage the child verbally and even ask a question or direct the child in a lessonlike manner. Children learn different cultural lessons depending on the kind of guidance they receive from their caregivers. The nonverbal style teaches children to watch and pick up appropriate behavior from their caregivers, and the verbal, direct style teaches children to be ready to answer questions and follow directions.

Sometimes the lessons caregivers are teaching are obvious, but at other times they may not be. Caregivers are often aware of the teaching purpose of activities that are typically thought of as learning situations; for example, when caregivers help a toddler put together a set of stacking rings or help an infant learn to squeeze a toy to make it squeak. However, caregivers may not be as aware of their teaching role in routine care-giving situations, such as when they are feeding an

infant or helping a toddler learn to self-feed. As Janet Gonzalez-Mena points out in her article, some cultural groups encourage self-feeding to help infants learn a sense of independence as early as possible. In other communities the caregiver's primary purpose may be to ensure that the child eats an adequate meal with a minimum amount of waste or mess. Caregivers often are not aware that they are teaching such cultural values.

One of the challenges facing caregivers in a multicultural world is to understand the culturally based lessons that they teach children through their actions and caregiving style. The following exercises are designed to help you recognize the many ways in which you influence children's learning throughout the day and to help you become less automatic in your interactions with children.

Exercise One: Analyze Activities and Routines

1. Make a list of the various play and routine caregiving activities that infants and toddlers are engaged in during a typical day.

2. For each activity, write down your purpose in setting up the activity or routine.

3. Discuss with another caregiver what you learned about the way you arranged the environment, activity, or routine. Go beyond thinking about the most obvious purpose, such as facilitating fine motor coordination through play with lego blocks, to ones that are more culturally or value based, are perhaps more subtle, and of which you are less conscious (e.g., encouraging independent problem solving as the child figures out how to take the blocks apart).

Exercise Two: Self-Observation

To recognize the manner in which you affect children's learning, try a self-observation exercise. When involved in an activity with an infant or toddler (e.g., when building a block tower or working a jack-in-the-box together), try to note mentally the role you are playing. What is the purpose behind your various actions? Jot down notes later. Keep the following questions in mind as you take mental notes:

1. Note when and how the child indicates a desire for assistance from you. How do you respond to the request? For example, do you encourage the child to try to complete the activity without help or do you immediately provide help? What kind of message does your response give to the child?

2. When you help a child, do you tend to do so verbally or nonverbally? Do you demonstrate actions for the child? Do you give explicit instructions or directions to the child? Do you take over the activity or let the child remain in charge?

3. How do you expect the child to respond to your help? Is it appropriate for the child to sit quietly and watch or listen to you? Or is it appropriate for the child to try a new action right away and learn from trial and error? Do you expect the child to be a cooperative partner with you or to be as independent of you as possible?

Remember that the purpose attached to a particular activity or behavior may vary for different cultural groups. In the same way that observing yourself gives you insight into your culturally based approach to learning, becoming a sensitive observer of children will give you insight into children's learning styles. Recognizing differences in learning styles and situations can help you be more responsive to individual children's needs and add to your repertoire of responsive caregiving skills. When you notice how children learn and pay attention to different learning styles, you can accommodate and respond to cultural differences in the same way you respond to individual differences.

When the children you are caring for are accustomed to a certain style of learning, be sensitive to each child's preferences and start out by supporting the child's way. Eventually, children can be encouraged to try alternative ways to learn. As long as the children are comfortable in trying out new approaches to learning, such experiences can be useful to them. Infants and toddlers are perceptive learners. Often, they become flexible and adjust well to expectations, routines, and practices in the child care program that differ from what they are accustomed to at home. The key to helping the child adapt is that the child's home culture is respected and appreciated and that the child feels comfortable and is supported in the child care setting. The caregiver's first step most often is to start with routines and practices familiar to the child. [My toddler has learned to manage many routines that are different from those she was accustomed to at home. For example, the toddler falls asleep by herself at her child care center but at home still needs to fall asleep in my arms.]

Conclusion

By taking part in activities that are important to their caregivers, children learn about the social and cultural values of the significant adults in their lives. Caregivers have a profound impact on children's learning as they convey their cultural values, beliefs, and attitudes to the children. Every aspect of the child care setting reflects the cultural experience of the caregivers who created the setting. Therefore, it is essential for caregivers of children from different cultural communities to understand and respect cultural differences. When caregivers become aware of their child-rearing goals, the skills they that emphasize, and their approach to learning and socialization, they can adapt to the home cultural experience of the children in their care. When a caregiver respects and adapts to a child, that child will be able to adapt to the caregiver and to the child care setting that the caregiver creates.

References

Cole, Michael, and Sheila Cole. 1989. *The Development of Children.* New York: W. H. Freeman and Co.

Heath, Shirley B. 1983. *Ways with Words: Language, Life, and Work in Communities and Classrooms.* New York: Cambridge University Press.

Rogoff, Barbara. 1991. *Apprenticeship in Thinking: Cognitive Development in Social Context.* New York: Oxford University Press, Inc.

Sorenson, E. Richard. 1979. "Early Tactile Communication and the Patterning of Human Organization: A New Guinea Case Study," in *Before Speech: The Beginning of Interpersonal Communication.* Edited by

Margaret Bullowa. New York: Cambridge University Press.

Springer, Robert. 1990. "The Pre-Kindergarten Educational Program: An Overview," *Kamehameha Journal of Education* (Center for Development of Early Education, Kamehameha Schools), Vol. 1 (May), 1–6.

Ward, Martha C. 1986. *Them Children: A Study in Language Learning.* New York: Holt, Rinehart, & Winston, 1971. Reprint, Prospect Heights, Ill.: Waveland Press, Inc.

Contrasting Cultural Practices

The following lists of contrasting cultural practices may help you identify and understand some of your own caregiving practices in relation to other culturally valid approaches:

Toilet training typically occurs when the child is physically mature and able to talk. The child learns through becoming increasingly independent.	Toilet training is introduced when the child is quite young (as young as one year old). The child learns through being cooperative in a partnership with the parent.
Children are provided with a scaled-down version of adult activities. During interactions in such activities, the parent adjusts speech and actions to the child's level of skill and understanding.	Children learn about adult activities by being present while adults go about their jobs and the household tasks. Children have the responsibility to learn culturally valued behaviors and practices by observing adults.
Adults have "conversations" with young infants. Adults endow the smallest vocalizations of the baby with meaning and intentionality and react to them emotionally. There is an emphasis on direct, verbal learning for infants.	Children learn language primarily through eavesdropping and observing through hours spent overhearing adults' conversations. Adults usually do not talk with young infants. There is an emphasis on nonverbal, observational learning for infants.
Babies spend a lot of time by themselves—sleeping in separate rooms and amusing themselves in playpens—and learn to use verbal communication to get the attention of adults; for example, by calling out to the parent or caregiver.	Babies are often in close physical contact with their parents or caregivers. They learn to use nonverbal communication, such as gestures with their hands or changes in muscle tone or posture, to get their needs met.
Adults encourage infants to learn self-feeding, even if that means making a mess.	During feeding, the adult's primary purpose may be to ensure that the child eats an adequate meal with a minimum amount of waste or mess.

Concerns of Immigrant Families

Alicia F. Lieberman

*I*mmigrant families often feel divided between two sets of emotions. On one hand they are sad about losing their country of origin and leaving behind family, friends, familiar ways of doing things, and the ease of communicating in their native language. On the other hand they are hopeful about the new opportunities that living in the United States brings and look forward to improving the quality of life for themselves and their children. These two sets of feelings often are in conflict because it is difficult to be simultaneously sad over a loss and hopeful about a new beginning. In addition, recently arrived immigrant families may be uncertain about their ability to succeed in their new country. Because of that uncertainty, their hope for a better future is mixed with fear that their wishes may not come true.

The attitudes that immigrants have about raising their children in a new and unfamiliar society reflect their different experiences. This article explores how the experiences of the parents may influence their responses to out-of-home child care and their behavior toward the child care provider.

Stress of Sudden Change

No matter how carefully people prepare to emigrate, the concrete act of crossing the border and arriving in the new country elicits a sudden experience of change. The experience becomes more acute as the immigrant realizes that the change is permanent.

Perhaps the most immediate and dramatic consequence of moving is the loss of one's language. Immigrants can no longer take for granted that what they say will be understood, and they often cannot understand what others tell them. One of the most basic certainties of being an adult—being able to communicate by

using speech—has been taken away. To make things worse, the loss occurs when the immigrant needs language the most because hundreds of facts must be learned and hundreds of new decisions must be made. For example, the immigrant needs to learn which areas of town are affordable, how to order and pay for utilities, how the transportation systems work, where and how to find child care, how to look for a job and fulfill the employer's expectations, and where and how to shop for the family's needs. All that in a new language! Unfamiliarity can be scary, and learning new things can be exhausting when the welfare of the whole family may depend on it.

When immigrants find that other people treat them respectfully and are tolerant of their mistakes, they feel welcome and confident that they have something of value to contribute. Unfortunately, immigrants unfamiliar with life in the United States often discover that people have little time or patience for them. In the United States success often depends on doing things quickly and well. Immigrants are still learning; therefore, they often do things slowly and with difficulty, such as counting their change at the counter or understanding directions. They may appear to be incompetent or ignorant, but they are trying to learn a whole new set of rules. When people treat them rudely or impatiently because of their awkwardness, immigrants may begin to think of themselves as incompetent or unable to learn. They may fear that others do not like them and lose faith in their ability to succeed.

These circumstances can take a toll on the mental health of immigrant families. Research shows that anxiety and depression are common experiences. However, most new arrivals become valuable members of society after an initial period of adjustment.

Longing for the Old Family Ways

Together with their wish to adapt, recent immigrants experience an intense longing for the way things were. The feeling is particularly strong in family relations. Many immigrants come from countries with traditional family organizations in which child care is provided by the mother, grandmother, or other trusted family or community members. That network is an important source of support, and parents do not need to worry about the quality of care their children receive.

Conditions are often quite different in the United States. When the extended family and familiar community are left behind, parents find themselves without a trusted support system for raising their children. If both parents need to work, young children have to be placed in the care of unfamiliar providers, who may belong to a different culture and who may not understand the recent immigrant's particular experiences and values.

A major disruption for immigrant families occurs when children learn the language, values, and social conventions of the new country faster than their parents do. The children are in infant care situations in which they see caregivers and children modeling different ways to do things. It is not uncommon for children as young as three years of age to be embarrassed by the imperfect English of their immigrant parents, to correct their parents' pronunciation, and to tell their parents how to say something in English. As the children grow older, they become the parents' guides to life in the United

States. Instead of the parents teaching the children, the children become the parents' teachers.

The reversal of roles can be an embarrassing situation, particularly when the parents are committed to the idea that adults always know best. In many cultures a strong cultural value holds that the adults carry the authority and that youths need to be respectful of and obedient to adults. That value is hard to maintain when the children see their parents as less knowledgeable in the new culture and begin to question the decisions and correct the behavior of their parents. For example, a three-year-old may complain because her parents do not allow her to spend the weekend with an American friend from child care. She may complain that "all the other children at child care do it." In that situation and other similar situations, the parents' mixed feelings about wanting to belong in the United States but longing for familiar ways of behavior may find expression in family tensions. Although the parents are proud that their children are learning how to act in the new country, they fear that their children will become too assimilated to

the United States and will grow up without knowing and respecting the values of their country of origin. That ambivalence is often expressed in the parents' relationship not only to their children but also to the child care providers.

Parents' Relationship to the Caregiver

The child care setting is where the children of immigrant families are most thoroughly exposed to the dominant values and traditions in the United States. The child care provider becomes the main teacher of those values and traditions not only for the child but also, sometimes, for the parents. Recently arrived parents learn a lot from observing the furnishings and decorations of the child care center, the food served, the games and activities offered, the caregivers' interactions with the children, the forms of discipline used, and the permitted and forbidden behaviors. From those sources the parents form an idea of the human and social values promoted by the child care providers. Often, in the parents' experience, those values become equated with the broader values of the dominant culture because the child care providers have authority and are central in much of the parents' and children's lives.

The parents often disagree with what they see taking place in the child care setting because the way in which the adults interact with the children clashes with the parents' cultural values. Sometimes parents are able to speak about their displeasure to the caregiver. In the best of cases, both parties can arrive at a friendly resolution of the problem, and the child care arrangement continues in a harmonious fashion. At other times the parents and the child care provider have such different outlooks that the parents decide to place their child elsewhere. In many situations the parents never express their displeasure openly because they are afraid of angering the provider and losing the child care. Instead, they may show their dissatisfaction indirectly by being sullen, not volunteering information about the child, bringing the child late, or failing to pick up the child at the appropriate time.

Culturally Different Child-Rearing Practices

Misunderstandings between caregivers and recent immigrant parents are often based on different cultural values about child rearing. Some cultural differences in child-rearing practices are discussed below.

Crying

Child care providers often view young children's crying as a form of communication that needs to be understood. Therefore, they often respond to crying with attempts to find out the reason for the child's distress and to alleviate it. Many cultures share that view. But in other cultures, crying that is not a result of hunger or pain is considered a sign that the child is spoiled or self-centered. Parents from those cultures tend to respond to the child's crying with scolding, ridicule, or other forms of punishment.

Example: The mother of a fifteen-month-old boy comes to pick him up at the end of the day and discovers that he is crying. The caregiver explains that the child seems to have missed his mother a lot that day and could not wait for her to arrive. The mother scolds the child, tells him that he knows she will pick him up, and says he is silly for crying.

Exploration

Members of the dominant American culture often place great value on curiosity and an interest in exploring. They consider the child's active manipulation of toys and vigorous physical activity healthy and natural ways of learning about the world.

Not all cultures share those attitudes. Some cultural groups believe that curiosity and active exploration are ill-mannered and rude and that children should be taught to be quiet and self-restrained rather than exuberant and spontaneous. In other cultures people place even more emphasis on freedom of physical movement than do people in the dominant culture in the United States. For members of those cultures, children's exuberance is not to be restricted. Some caregivers in the United States may find themselves responding to those children as though they were hyperactive and uncontrollable.

Example: The mother of a ten-month-old baby complains to the caregiver that the baby is allowed to crawl all over the classroom. She tells the caregiver that at home the baby stays in a playpen to keep her safe and quiet. She adds that lately the baby has started complaining about being put in the playpen because she is getting used to roaming freely in child care. The mother does not like the situation.

Example: The father of a two-year-old girl brings her to child care and laughs with pleasure when she tries to climb on the shelves of the bookcase. The caregiver tells the child that the bookcase is not for climbing. The father complains that the caregiver is being overly strict and that the child will not hurt herself or damage the bookcase by climbing on it. He explains that children need freedom to explore so that they will not grow up to be shy or afraid.

Anger

Child development experts in the United States commonly consider a child's anger a normal reaction to frustration. Efforts to help the child manage anger focus on finding forms of expression that will not hurt either the child or others. The goal is not to suppress anger but to show it in socially acceptable ways.

Members of many other cultures believe that Americans are too permissive in their acceptance of anger. They believe that politeness is a more important value than the expression of negative emotions. In those cultures children are taught to suppress their anger, and failure to do so is regarded with severe disapproval.

Example: Two boys two and one-half years old begin to struggle over a toy. One of them hits the other. The caregiver tells the child that hitting is not allowed and that he should have some quiet time. The child screams that he does not want quiet time and throws himself on the

floor, kicking and screaming. The caregiver talks soothingly to him to calm him down but reminds him that he did something that is not allowed. A parent who is watching the scene feels that the caregiver is being too patient. The parent advises the caregiver to yell at the child and tell him that the caregiver will stop loving him if he misbehaves again.

Expression of Feelings

In the dominant culture in the United States, speaking about feelings rather than acting on them is considered a sign of emotional maturity. Therefore, children are taught to express their feelings in words. Child care providers help children do so by speaking for them when the children themselves cannot do it. A child care provider may say, for example, "It makes you sad when Mommy leaves," "You got angry when Sarah took your doll from you," or "You sure are enjoying that ice cream."

Other cultures place much less reliance on language to express feelings. Sometimes feelings are expressed through action more readily than through words. For example, a person's cultural pattern may be to hug and kiss a lot rather than

say "I love you" or to express anger through a quick slap on the hand rather than express the anger verbally. In that culture teaching a child to speak about feelings may be considered too intellectual or artificial.

People in yet other cultures place much value on not showing emotion. They may carefully screen their words and actions to avoid showing how they are feeling. In those cultures teaching children to put feelings into words may be quite undesirable.

Example: A little girl is crying because she does not want her mother to leave. The caregiver says, "You are sad that mommy is leaving. You want mommy to stay, don't you?" The mother feels that such talk only encourages the child to cry more. She believes the caregiver should take the child to the play yard and help her forget about the separation instead of talking about it.

Gender-Based Expectations

Expectations based on gender is a topic of some debate in the United States. A traditional tendency has been to think of girls as "sugar and spice and everything nice" and to consider boys similar to "snakes and snails and puppy dog tails." Girls were expected to live up to the stereotype by being sweet and compliant, and boys were expected to be rowdy and full of mischief. The emergence of feminism led to considerable pressure to believe that girls and boys are born equal in temperament and are shaped by society to acquire the traits culturally associated with femininity or masculinity.

The pendulum has now swung back and rests somewhere between the two positions. People generally acknowledge that some differences may be biologically innate, but most people also

accept that social perceptions and cultural values shape one's views of how boys and girls should behave. Usually, American child care providers try not to treat boys and girls differently. They encourage children of both sexes to acquire a wide range of skills and to engage in many different kinds of activities.

More traditional cultures retain a strong conviction that boys and girls need to be treated differently. Members of those cultures may be shocked to see a girl engage in boisterous physical activity, speak loudly, get in rough-and-tumble play with a boy, or pretend she is a firefighter. The same people may worry if they see boys playing with dolls or pretending to cook. The atmosphere of a regular American child care setting may be quite upsetting for parents with those values because of the worry that their children might not grow up to be "real" boys or "proper" girls by the parents' cultural standards.

Example: The father of a three-year-old girl is upset when she runs up to him with a toy fire engine and announces that she will be a firefighter when she grows up. He tells her that girls cannot be firefighters but that she can be a nurse instead.

Example: The mother of a two-year-old boy complains that the child is playing with his sister's doll at home—feeding it and putting it to sleep. She explains to him that women do that, not boys, but he persists. She asks the caregiver not to let him play with dolls in child care.

Curiosity About the Body

In some cultural groups people have become increasingly used to the idea that it is natural and healthy for young children to be interested in their bodies, to be curious about the differences between boys and girls, and to touch their private parts occasionally. It is common for children in group care to see each other's genitals in the process of diapering or toilet training. Children's questions about genital differences are usually answered directly and matter of factly. When the children grow older and become interested in reproduction, their questions about the topic are also answered truthfully. But children do not usually see adults naked. When they do, the experience almost always occurs at home and because the child has access to the bathroom when the parents are using it.

There are great cultural differences in learning about the human body. Some immigrants come from cultures in which sexual topics are taboo and children are punished if they touch themselves. Bodily privacy is strictly respected, and parents go to great lengths to make sure children are as old as possible before they discover the facts of gender differences or reproduction. For those people more permissive ways are quite shocking and distasteful.

In other cultures people are quite open about discussing sexual matters; and nudity between children and adults occurs in accepted social activities, such as the use of the sauna in Scandinavian countries. For members of those cultures, distaste for casual nudity in the home may appear prudish and old-fashioned.

Example: The father of an eighteen-month-old girl complains that boys and girls see each other during toileting at child care. He complains that the child is now touching herself at home and asking for the names of her private parts in their native language. The father says that girls need to be modest and that he does not like her growing curiosity about her body.

Example: A three-year-old boy describes in great detail how the whole family takes showers together and how they like to swim naked in the river. The child also makes drawings of naked adults. The other children feel uncomfortable with his talk. The caregiver later talks with the mother, who says that nudity is quite natural and that she does not want her child to be inhibited by it.

Physical Punishment

Many people, even some in the United States, still believe that spanking or other forms of physical punishment are acceptable ways of disciplining children. However, in the fields of child care, childhood education, and child psychology, the belief is well established that physical punishment is not an effective form of teaching children how to behave. Experts agree that physical punishment may make children more aggressive and more likely to misbehave when nobody is watching. For that reason child care providers do not spank children or use other forms of physical punishment. Instead, they resort to such techniques as explain-

ing to the child what he or she did wrong, showing disapproval or disappointment, redirecting the child's behavior, or using time out.

In other cultures, however, physical punishment is the preferred form of discipline. The severity of the punishment may range from relatively slight, such as tapping the hand when the child touches a forbidden object, to severe, such as hitting with a belt hard enough to leave marks—an act that would be considered reportable child abuse in the United States.

When there are basic differences in beliefs about punishment between the parents and the caregiver, serious conflict is likely to result. The child care provider may feel compelled to confront the parents in order to protect the child. In severe situations the caregiver may even decide to report the parents to the child protection services. However, the parents may feel that they did nothing wrong and that they are the targets of cultural discrimination.

It is important to remember that physical punishment that leaves marks, such as bruises, on the child's body is *illegal* in the United States. Even though some cultures allow that kind of punishment, parents need to know that in the United States, *they may not use it.* In moving to the United States, parents agree to learn and obey the laws of their new country, even when those laws are different from the customs of their home country. If parents break the child abuse laws, the caregiver needs to report the parents regardless of cultural practices.

Example of physical punishment: An eighteen-month-old child puts a wooden block in his mouth. His mother tells him not to do it. The child complies, but a little later does it again. The mother slaps his hand and says, "No."

Example of physical abuse: A three-year-old child comes to child care with bruises on his legs. When the caregiver asks what happened, the child says, "My uncle hit me with a belt."

Tips for Successful Communication with Immigrant Parents

1. *Remember the language difference.* Try speaking slowly and clearly to make the non-English-speaking parent feel more competent. Use short, simple sentences and uncomplicated words.

2. *Explain the child care routine.* Do not take for granted that the parent knows or understands the rules of the child care setting. Immigrant families often take some time to adjust to the rules because they come from countries in which expectations about punctuality, nutrition, or bodily care may be different.

3. *Acknowledge tension and think about the reasons for it.* If there seems to be tension between the parent and yourself, do not take it as a personal offense. Think for a while about what is bothering you or what seems to upset the parent. Ask yourself whether cultural differences might be contributing to the feeling.

4. *Ask questions about the family's child rearing.* When you do not understand some behavior, do not be shy about asking how things are done in the parents' home country. Tell them you know that people from different countries raise their children differently and you want to understand how they do things. That way of framing the differences will help the parent know you do not think of your child-rearing methods as good and their methods as bad. Your request for information will also let them know you are interested in learning about and accepting their lifestyle.

5. *Serve as a cultural bridge between the parents' culture and the culture of child care.* Try to educate the parents about the way things are done in child

care. Remember that you may be the only bridge the parents have with the larger society and the only person with the knowledge and understanding to help the parents adjust.

6. *Remember that you are an authority figure.* You are not only a source of knowledge but also an authority figure. The parents are likely to respect what you say but probably are also a little afraid of you. For them you are a symbol of the American institutions. They want your approval of their children and of themselves and are afraid of your disapproval.

7. *Establish a trusting atmosphere that encourages dialogue.* If you feel the parents are doing something wrong with their children, try to establish a climate of trust and acceptance before you bring up the subject. Try to discuss the problem in ways that express care and concern rather than anger and disapproval. That approach will help relieve the parents' anxiety about displeasing you. If the parents are not anxious, they will be more likely to hear what you are saying and not worry about how to defend themselves.

8. *Give constructive feedback.* If the child's behavior worries you, try to think also of the child's strengths. That approach will help you put the problem in the context of the child's overall development. When you talk with the parents, start by telling them about the delightful parts of the child's personality and about the things he or she does well. Bring up the source of worry as another area of the child's functioning that you want to discuss, making sure you refer back to the child's strengths as well. Doing so will help the parents know that you like

their child and help them not to feel hopeless or angry with themselves, their child, or you.

Summary

Above all remember that migration is a source of great stress for a family. Feelings of personal competence and self-esteem are severely threatened by the loss of culture, language, and support systems and by the need to relearn basic skills. Anxiety and depression are common. Immigrants see their children as a source of hope for helping them belong in the new country. They look to the child care provider as a person who will help them realize that hope. You are in the unique position of helping the families feel that their own culture is rich and valuable and that there are many satisfactions in adjusting to life in the United States.

References

Erikson, Erik H. [1950] 1993. *Childhood and Society*. New York: W. W. Norton and Co., Inc.

Garcia Coll, Cynthia T. 1990. "Developmental Outcome of Minority Infants: A Process-Oriented Look into Our Beginnings," *Child Development*, Vol. 61 (April), 270–89.

Lieberman, Alicia F. 1989. "What Is Culturally Sensitive Intervention?" *Early Child Development and Care,* Vol. 50 (September), 197–204.

Spencer, Margaret B. 1990. "Development of Minority Children: An Introduction," *Child Development*, Vol. 61 (April), 267–69.

Section Three:
The Process of Culturally
Sensitive Care

Developing Culturally Responsive Caregiving Practices: Acknowledge, Ask, and Adapt

Louise Derman-Sparks

We need all the different kinds of people we can find
To make freedom's dream come true.
So as I learn to like the differences in me,
I learn to like the differences in you.

—Bill Martin, Jr., *I Am Freedom's Child*

Those lines from the wonderful children's book *I Am Freedom's Child* capture the underlying vision of culturally responsive caregiving. That is what this article is about: how to learn to like the differences in me and in you. In the learning process you will acquire a set of skills that will enable you to support children's and adults' identities and their way of being in the world.

Everyone needs to learn how to be culturally responsive. As Carol Brunson Phillips explains in her article, the various rules of your own culture that you learn as you grow up become the basis for how you see, organize, and interpret your experiences and what you value or dislike. But different cultures teach people different rules. Not all people interpret or value the same things in the same way. How,

then, do caregivers sensitively support the growth of infants and toddlers who are growing up in families whose cultural beliefs about children and child rearing are different from their own? That is the challenge each caregiver must take on.

To be culturally responsive, you do not need to know beforehand everything there is to know about the cultures of all the children with whom you work. Therefore, this article is not a lesson on the cultures of different ethnic groups in the United States. Instead, you will learn how to *find out* what you need to know to care sensitively for each child in your care and how to use the information in your work. Keep in mind that becoming culturally responsive is an ongoing learning process. Every new situation—a new child and family, a new caregiving setting, a new staff member—requires that you use cul-

---

The epigraph is reprinted by permission of SRA/Macmillan/McGraw-Hill, School Publishing Co.

turally responsive strategies to gain the knowledge and develop the practices necessary for that situation.

Everyone in a caregiving relationship benefits from culturally responsive practices. For example:

- *Caregivers* gain a better understanding of themselves and an expanded, richer, more powerful awareness of the complexities of how children develop and learn. The knowledge allows caregivers more effectively to meet the needs of all the children and families with whom they work.

- *Parents and other family members* are better able to build the trusting partnerships with the child care staff that are essential for working on problems together. Caregivers can also more fully support effective parenting at home.

- *Children* gain a deeper sense of security and predictability in their lives, conditions that are essential for emotional and cognitive development.

Working through Thinking/Doing Activity 1 at the end of this article will help you explore the benefits of experiencing cultural differences.

The Learning Process

The culturally responsive learning process involves three tasks:

1. Becoming consciously aware of one's own cultural beliefs and values about how children develop and how best to nurture and raise them
2. Practicing strategies for discovering other people's cultural assumptions about child development and child-rearing methods
3. Learning and practicing problem-solving strategies for negotiating and

resolving conflicts caused by cultural differences

The first task means recognizing that you act on your assumptions about children and child rearing, even though you may not consciously think about them. When you do "what comes naturally" (or even what you learned in training), you are acting out a set of cultural values and rules. You are using them to judge what is normal, what is right, or what is best. However, doing what comes naturally to you may not always be best for a particular child because your actions may conflict with another set of beliefs and rules about child rearing. Generally, as caregiver you become aware of your cultural assumptions when you experience a cultural conflict in a caregiving situation. Task one requires that you become aware of the assumptions, stereotypes, and biases that you learned about other cultural groups as you grew up.

The second task means finding out about the child-rearing goals, beliefs, and practices of every family and staff member with whom you work. While you go

program to meet the children's culturally based needs.

Remember that becoming culturally responsive is a learning process that never ends. The more practice you have, the better you get at it; but you always have something new to learn about yourself and other people. The process takes time and patience.

Becoming culturally responsive also builds on your human capacity to connect with other people across cultural differences. Your shared humanness is the bridge. Characteristics such as openness, curiosity, caring, willingness to learn and to change, and a sense of humor help make the learning process work.

See Thinking/Doing Activities 2 and 3 at the end of this article.

Acknowledge, Ask, and Adapt

By putting into practice the following steps for culturally responsive caregiving, you will gain the information you need to support appropriately the growth of all the children in your care.

Step 1: Acknowledge

The first step is a step of recognition in which you use your growing awareness of the existence of different cultural assumptions about infant and toddler development. A willingness to be open with yourself is essential to the success of this step.

a. Acknowledge to yourself that a cultural difference or conflict may exist between you and a parent in a particular aspect of caregiving. You may become aware of a significant cultural difference from a parent's reaction to an interaction between you and his or her child; from a child's response of

about doing that, keep in mind that families from the same ethnic background do not all express their culture in the same way in their daily lives. Different families may be at different points on a scale of being very traditional to being like the dominant American culture. Furthermore, even families at the same point on the scale may act out their cultural beliefs in different ways. As you make efforts to understand each child's behavior within his or her cultural context, beware of slipping into the assumption that different behavior is not normal. To avoid culturally insensitive responses, you must first assume you are seeing normal development until you gather more information.

The third task in the culturally responsive learning process means building skills in communicating with staff and families about cultural issues. This task requires practice. You need to state your ideas clearly, negotiate solutions that resolve particular cultural conflicts, and adapt the caregiving practices in your discomfort, confusion, or anxiety; or from information you get from a parent or another caregiver about the cultural child-rearing practices of the child's family. Check your feelings; be careful not to make a quick judgment that the parent's way is wrong.

b. Let the parents or another family member know that there is an issue you need to discuss. Show your respect for the family by the caring manner in which you acknowledge the need to talk together.

Step 2: Ask

The second step is an information-gathering step. The goal is to get the information you need about the parents' and your cultural beliefs and values so that you can solve the problem together during the third step. Do not rush the second step.

a. Find out how the parents or other family members view and feel about the issue that concerns you and how they would handle the caregiving situation. To do that, ask questions and watch the interactions between the child and family member in the child care setting and, if possible, interactions at the child's home.

b. Spell out to yourself your cultural beliefs about the best way to handle the situation. Ask yourself how you feel about the parent's viewpoint and practice. Are you uncomfortable because the viewpoint is contrary to your basic cultural beliefs about caregiving? Or are you comfortable with the parent's viewpoint, even though it is different from your own?

Step 3: Adapt

In this last problem-solving step, you use the information gathered in step two to resolve conflicts caused by cultural differences and find the most effective way to support each child's growth.

a. *Communicate.* Clarify the issue. Work together with family members to develop strategies and decide how best to resolve the situation. It is important that you want to have a joint solution.

b. *Negotiate.* In discussion all parties suggest various ideas and explore together the strengths and weaknesses of each idea. Try to discover the bottom line for each of you (solutions that would be possible for either party to live with).

c. *Resolve.* Come to an agreement on the best action to take in the situation. Several resolutions are possible: (1) the caregiver and parent may agree to follow the solution preferred by the parent to maintain consistency with the family's child rearing; (2) both parties may agree to an action that is a modification of what the caregiver and parent do; or (3) the parent may come

to understand why the caregiver uses a particular action and end up accepting it.

Sometimes, even with sensitive use of the acknowledge, ask, and adapt steps, it may not be possible to resolve a particular cultural conflict. Legal regulations for the program may interfere with a solution satisfactory to the family (although, even then, some compromise may be found that will satisfy the regulations and meet some of the family's needs). Resolution may also be impossible if the caregiver's bottom line about an issue will not allow any modifications in how he or she works with the infant or toddler. When that is the case, the caregiver needs to do *much* soul searching about his or her beliefs and sensitively share those thoughts with the parents before refusing to make any changes.

If the process of communication and negotiation has been done with car-ing, even though a problem cannot be completely resolved, families will at least know that the caregiver tried. However, a family may decide that their child would be better cared for in another child care setting that will be more culturally consistent for them. Occasionally, a caregiver in a center may decide to go to another program because the caregiver does not feel she or he can meet the cultural requirements of a particular group of families.

Assessing Cultural Responsiveness

The following scenarios of caregiving situations that have occurred in child care settings illustrate how to use the acknowledge, ask, and adapt steps. After each example the caregiver's use of the three steps receives a rating. See whether you agree or disagree with those ratings.

Scenario 1: A Baby Crying

As you read the different ways Joan, the caregiver, handles the situation, think about how you would rate her behavior.

The Situation

Rosy, six months old, is waking up from her nap and begins to cry. Joan, her caregiver, has begun to dress Mark. She lets Rosy cry while she finishes dressing Mark (which takes about five minutes), then picks Rosy up. In the meantime Rosy's mother (Mrs. H) has come early to pick up her daughter and sees the incident. When Joan greets her, Mrs. H takes Rosy from her and holds Rosy tightly. Rosy does not come to child care the next two days. When Joan calls to find out what has happened, Mrs. H says that Rosy will be back the next day, but she does not return until the following Monday. By then, Joan is concerned. On the day Rosy returns, Joan takes Mrs. H aside and asks why Rosy was out so long. Mrs. H replies, "Rosy was upset. You didn't take good care of her."

Response X

Joan is surprised and hurt. She feels she has taken good care of Rosy. She replies: "I take good care of all my babies. I would never do anything to hurt Rosy." Mrs. H: "Last time, you let her cry too much." Joan thinks back to Rosy's last day: "I was dressing Mark. I only let Rosy cry a few minutes." Mrs. H: "You waited too long." Joan, a little annoyed: "No, I didn't. I had to take care of Mark first. Besides, it doesn't hurt a baby to cry a little." Mrs. H insists: "That's not good. In my country, we always pick up the baby right away."

By now Joan is really annoyed: "Mrs. H, in this country we do not believe in spoiling babies. It's good for Rosy to learn that an adult won't always come immediately when she cries." Mrs. H looks upset but does not say any more.

Joan decides that she has to do something at the center to ensure that Rosy does not become too spoiled. She starts to let Rosy cry a little longer before she goes to her so that Rosy can learn to wait. Rosy begins to cry more often when her mother leaves her in the morning. Joan sees that as evidence of Mrs. H's "overprotection" and continues with her plan of teaching Rosy to wait. Rosy is not doing as well, so Joan decides to speak with Mrs. H again to find out what is going wrong at home.

Rating: Response X is culturally repressive.

Step 1: *Acknowledge* gets a minus.
Joan pays attention only to her own feelings and acts defensively by trying to justify herself. She acknowledges neither Rosy's mother's concern nor that there is a problem.

Step 2: *Ask* gets a minus.
Joan does not try to find out anything about what is behind Mrs. H's concern. Nor does she show any evidence of recognizing that her own cultural assumptions are only one way of thinking about the issue.

Instead, she makes a quick judgment that Mrs. H must be spoiling Rosy.

Step 3: *Adapt* gets a minus.
Joan makes no effort to adapt her behavior to Rosy's family's cultural beliefs and behaviors and makes things worse for Rosy by creating an even wider gap between what Rosy's family does at home and what she, Joan, does to avoid spoiling Rosy. When Rosy shows signs of not thriving at the center, Joan again assumes the cause must be a problem at home. Joan does not use good communication, negotiation, or conflict resolution skills.

Response Y

Joan is surprised and concerned. She thought that Rosy's mother trusted her. Joan: "Mrs. H, I'm sorry you feel that way. I care very much about Rosy and do not want to hurt her in any way." Mrs. H: "Last time you let her cry too long." Joan: "I had to finish dressing Mark, and she didn't sound too upset. I was going to pick her up shortly." Mrs. H: "That's too long. That's not good for babies." Joan: "What do you do at home when Rosy starts to cry?" Mrs. H: "In my house we pick her up right away. That is good for babies."

Joan: "Well, that may work for you at home, but in child care we can't always do that. There are other babies who need care also. It won't hurt Rosy to cry a few minutes. In fact, it will be good for her. You don't want her to be spoiled." Mrs. H shakes her head: "In my country we do not think that is good for babies." By now Joan is unhappy. She does not like having a disagreement with a parent but she does not want to give in. Joan: "At home you can pick her up as you think best, but in child care she will have to get used to waiting sometimes."

When Joan notices that Mrs. H has become more distant and that Rosy cries more often when her mother leaves her, she begins to think that Rosy is confused by being handled one way at home and another way in child care. She decides to work with Mrs. H to convince her to let Rosy cry a little longer at home before picking her up.

Rating: Response Y is partly culturally responsive, partly culturally repressive.

Step 1: *Acknowledge* gets a plus.
Joan recognizes that Rosy's mother is upset and expresses concern about how she is feeling.

Step 2: *Ask* gets a plus for one part, a minus for another part.
Joan gets a plus for asking for some information and for realizing that Rosy's mother's belief about how to handle crying differs from her own. She gets a minus because she moves too quickly to a solution—she does not get sufficient information from Mrs. H to determine the seriousness of the difference.

Step 3: *Adapt* gets a minus.
Joan is not willing to change her behavior at all in the child care setting. She thinks of that as giving in rather than as adapting. When Rosy is not doing well in child care, Joan thinks Mrs. H should change how she handles crying at home. Joan does not think about how her own behavior might have made Mrs. H uneasy and may be making Rosy feel more insecure in the child care program. Because Joan does not use step three, the consequence of

response Y is culturally repressive, even though Joan used the first two steps.

Response Z

Joan realizes immediately that this is a serious issue. Rosy's mother has never disagreed with or criticized the caregivers before. Joan: "Mrs. H, I care very much for Rosy and do not want to hurt her in any way. Please tell me what I did that you think wasn't good for her." Mrs. H: "You let her cry too long last time she was here." Joan: "When I was dressing Mark?" Mrs. H nods her head yes. Joan: "What would you have done?" Mrs. H: "I would have picked her up right away." Joan: "Sounds as though picking up a crying baby right away is very important to you." Mrs. H: "In my country we think a mother who lets her baby cry is not good." Joan: "So when I didn't pick Rosy up right away, it worried you." Mrs. H nods again: "Yes, Rosy will be frightened." Joan: "Is that why you kept her home the past few days?" Mrs. H: "I wanted her home with me. But now I have to go back to work."

Joan: "I know it is hard for you to leave Rosy here all day, especially if you think I was doing something that would upset her. I had not known that what seemed to me like letting Rosy cry only a little while seemed too long to you. Now that I understand how you feel and what you do, I will be more careful about picking her up as soon as she cries. Will that make you feel safer leaving her here?" Mrs. H smiles: "Yes."

Joan: "I also need to tell you that because other babies need attention in child care, and sometimes there is only one adult free, once in a while Rosy may have to wait a little to be picked up. That might happen if another baby is in physical danger or is hurt and I am the only adult available. Will you be comfortable with that?" Mrs. H: "I know there are other babies. I just want to know that Rosy will be safe."

Joan: "I'm so glad you let me know that you were unhappy with what I did. Please be sure to let me know if anything else I do bothers you. That way we will make sure that Rosy gets the best care I can give her." Mrs. H: "You tell me also if there is something I need to know."

After the conversation with Rosy's mother, Joan realizes she has not thought much about what the parents of her other babies, who come from a number of different ethnic groups, think about how to handle crying. She also wonders if other mothers from the same ethnic background as Mrs. H feel the same way as Mrs. H. She decides to ask each family about their views when they pick up their babies during the following week. She also decides that a newsletter about different families' ideas about handling crying and a parents meeting might help parents understand that different children may need different kinds of responses for them to feel secure in child care.

Rating: Response Z is culturally responsive.

Step 1: *Acknowledge* gets a plus.
   Joan immediately makes clear that she is open to hearing about what upset Rosy's mother. She also responds to Mrs. H's feelings. Joan shows that she is not defensive about making mistakes; instead, she accepts that she does and wants to learn more so that she can do better.

Step 2: *Ask* gets a plus.
   Joan asks questions that help get her

the kind of information she needs to understand why Mrs. H is upset. (Joan learns not only how Mrs. H handles crying but also that her definition of being a good mother depends on her response.)

Step 3: *Adapt* gets a plus.

Joan is willing to modify her behavior to be more consistent with Mrs. H's behavior. She does that for Rosy's sake (so Rosy will feel secure), for Mrs. H's sake (so Mrs. H will feel secure leaving Rosy at child care), and for her own sake (so she will continue a trusting relationship with Mrs. H). Mrs. H also has to do a little adapting because Joan lets her know that once in a while she may not be able to pick Rosy up immediately when she cries. Joan also recognizes that she needs more information from the rest of the parents and makes a plan for getting it. That behavior indicates that Joan is not defensive about not knowing everything; instead, she is comfortable in planning how to get the information she needs when she discovers that she needs it.

See Thinking/Doing Activity 4 at the end of this article.

Scenario 2: Babies Wearing Protective Amulets

Five staff members in an infant/toddler center try to decide what to do about a cultural practice of some families that conflicts with one of the center's regulations. Each staff person represents one kind of response to the problem. As you read their discussion, think about which solutions you consider culturally repressive and which culturally responsive. Which solution would you choose? Or would you create a solution different from those mentioned?

The Situation

Five of the families in the center come from an ethnic group whose cultural practice is to have babies wear a protective amulet around the neck. The amulets have an important religious significance; the families believe the amulets protect their babies against illnesses and other dangers. However, the child care center regulation states that infants and toddlers may not wear necklaces for safety reasons. Injuries may be caused by other babies pulling the necklaces too tight or yanking them off or by the babies chewing on them and choking. The amulets might also be lost.

Staff Discussion

Rosa: I think we have a real problem here. I asked Mrs. M about the amulet, and she said she never takes it off. The baby could come to harm if she did.

Harriet: Boy, what superstition. I don't think we should give in to it. It's very simple—wearing a necklace is against the regulations. Besides, we know that taking off the amulet will not hurt the baby.

Mark: We may not think it will; but if the families think so, they will be very unhappy and anxious if we remove the amulets.

Lynn: Well, I don't see what else we can do. I mean, I feel sympathy for the families' feelings, but we cannot let the kids wear them—it's too dangerous.

Rosa: I agree that it could be dangerous, but I don't think we can just ask the families to take them off.

Harriet: Well, I think we are making a big deal out of nothing. Families have to accept the rules when they use the center. Besides, I don't think we should be encouraging such practices. They are living in America now.

Rosa: They are not *your* religious beliefs, but they *are* the families' beliefs. They are as important to them as yours are to you.

Lynn: Let's just tell them we are sorry, but it is not safe and it is against the rules. We can say their children can wear the amulets at home and

	reassure them that we have other ways to keep the babies safe and healthy at the center.
Mark:	I think we need to do more. We have to consider the children's safety from both our point of view and the families' point of view.
Harriet:	If we don't follow the regulations, we will be out of compliance.
Rosa:	We need to find solutions that deal with the regulations and also meet the families' needs. I can think of one. I am sure we can think of others. I suggest that we ask parents to take off the amulets when they come to the center and put them in a special box that we will keep on a shelf in the room. When their child goes home, they can put the amulet back on.
Mark:	I think we need to ask the families if that will be enough. If it isn't, we need other ideas. What if we suggest pinning the amulet to the underside of the child's shirt so that it is still on the child but cannot be pulled?
Rosa:	We might also suggest that the baby can wear the amulet if it fits securely around the neck—not too tight and not loose enough to be pulled.
Lynn:	That last suggestion would be going against the regulations.
Mark:	I think we sometimes have to consider modifying regulations to meet families' needs. If the parents don't feel that their child is safe, we will not be able to build a trusting relationship with them, even if we know our regulation is intended for the children's safety.
Harriet:	I will not agree to a solution that goes against the regulation.
Rosa:	I think we first need to talk with the families before we decide among ourselves which solution to use. They may have other ideas of their own. I think we can find a solution that fits the intent of the regulation.
Mark:	In raising this issue with parents, I suggest we do three things: one, explain our safety concerns to the families—how, in the center, where

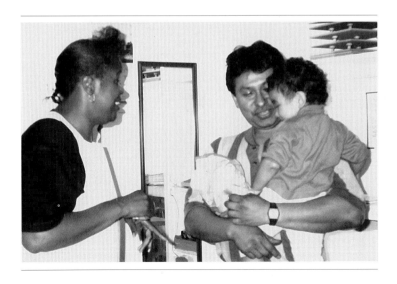

many babies and toddlers are playing with each other, necklaces like the amulets can cause injuries. We should explain what those injuries could be and how accidents can happen quickly, even when adults, who may be paying attention to other babies or toddlers, are around. Two, we should ask more about the importance of the amulets and assure the parents that we empathize with their viewpoint. Three, we should suggest some of the possible options and find out what other ideas they have. Then, together, we can figure out what solutions will be acceptable to them and to us.

Rosa and Mark volunteer to meet with the five families and report back to the rest of the staff.

Ratings

Harriet is culturally repressive. She does not use any of the culturally responsive steps. Because she refuses to acknowledge that there is a problem, she does not even consider asking the parents about their beliefs. Lastly, she is not willing to consider any solution except to remove the amulets.

Lynn is culturally repressive. She shows more feeling for the families than Harriet does (Lynn acknowledges a problem), but she is not interested in learning about the parents' beliefs and is not willing to make any changes to meet their needs. She sees the safety of the children only from the center's perspective.

Mark and *Rosa* are culturally responsive. They know how to use the acknowledge, ask, and adapt steps to work on resolving a problem. They want to communicate and work with the parents to find a solution that respects the families' beliefs and also meets the safety requirements of the center. Mark is more willing than Rosa to modify the regulations, if necessary.

See Thinking/Doing Activity 5 at the end of the article to examine your responses to this kind of situation.

In this scenario a cultural belief of several families conflicts with the caregiver's educational principles.

The Situation

Several families in the center strongly believe that keeping their toddlers clean and neat during the day demonstrates caring and the teaching of healthy behavior on the part of the caregiver. At home, whenever the toddlers get messy or dirty, an adult immediately cleans them. The caregiver believes an essential part of children's healthy development is for children to participate actively with materials such as sand, water, and paint, to feed themselves, and so forth. That means that toddlers do get messy. She also believes that toddlers should help clean themselves. The caregiver does help them clean up at points during the day (after an activity is over, before eating, and before a nap); but if she cleaned every child as soon as he or she got messy, the caregiver would be spending most of her time cleaning up. She does not think that is necessary.

How do *you* think the caregiver should handle the situation? Jot down your ideas for each step.

Step 1: Acknowledge

What could the caregiver say to herself and to the parents to communicate her awareness that this is a problem that they need to solve jointly?

Step 2: Ask

What questions could the caregiver ask the parents to get information that will help her understand more precisely the parents' concerns and what they think is an appropriate practice?

Step 3: Adapt

How can the caregiver open a negotiation with the parents about what to do? The caregiver does not want to stop children from being active with materials or stop them from learning how to take care of themselves. How can the caregiver explain why she allows children to get messy without immediately cleaning them and also communicate that she wants to find ways to meet the parents' needs? What modifications of child care practice might the caregiver explore with the parents? What is fair to expect parents to accept as modification of their home behaviors while their children are at the center?

Look over your notes as you consider the following questions for each step.

Acknowledge:

- Have you examined your feelings about the issue?
- Are you assuming before you talk with the parents that their requests about cleanliness will interfere with your program or with the toddlers' development?
- Will the parents understand that you want to resolve this cultural difference with them? (If you just state your program's policy without opening a

discussion, you are not using culturally responsive communication for this step.)

Ask:

- Have you asked the kind of questions that will give you the information you need to understand why parents think it is important for their toddler to stay clean (i.e., their beliefs about children playing with messy materials)?
- Are your questions supportive so that parents will feel comfortable answering them?

Adapt:

- Have you clarified the situation in a way that invites parents to resolve *with*

you how their child can participate in a full range of activities?
- Have you shown openness to finding a way to meet the parents' needs for cleanliness and neatness while being clear about your educational beliefs? For example, you might decide to add more opportunities during the day in which you help the toddlers get clean. If you are in a center, you might get a washing machine so that clothes that are especially dirty can be washed before the children go home. (These are examples only, not necessarily what *you* would do.)

See Thinking/Doing Activity 6 at the end of this article.

Developmental Issues or Cultural Differences?

When caregivers are not sensitive to cultural differences, they may interpret a baby's or toddler's healthy behavior as a developmental issue. Therefore, another important part of practicing culturally responsive caregiving is knowing when a child's behavior does suggest a developmental problem and is not a culturally different way of exhibiting normal development. Generally, a particular behavior of a child will qualify as a developmental problem when it is seen as a problem in the child's culture as well. Use the acknowledge, ask, and adapt steps here, too, to determine whether you are dealing with a cultural difference or a developmental issue.

Determine the Nature of the Behavior

1. Identify specifically what concerns you about the child's behavior, given your knowledge about infant/toddler development.
2. Gather information from other sources about the behavior that concerns you; for example, talk to the staff in your center, other family child care providers, specialists in infant/toddler and child development, and individuals knowledgeable about the culture of the family.
3. Respectfully communicate with the child's parents about the behavior of concern and ask for their help in understanding what the behavior means. Keep in mind that the *same* behavior may be all right in one cultural context and signal a problem in another. For example, a two-year-old who expects to be fed by an adult may be showing culturally appropriate behavior in one family and be considered too dependent in another. Therefore, the child's parents are an important source of information in your effort to understand the relationship between the home culture and the child's developmental progress.

- Ask parents whether they see the same behavior at home and, if they do, what they think about it.
- If the parents express no concern about the behavior, ask questions that help you understand why it does not concern them. Their response may help you realize that you are observing a cultural difference.
- If the parents say the behavior worries them, ask questions that help you understand *why* it worries them and what they think is causing the problem.

Work Toward a Solution

What you do after collecting all the information depends on whether you decide that the child's behavior reflects a cultural difference or is indicative of a developmental issue. If the behavior reflects a cultural difference, you can proceed as recommended in the previous scenarios. If the behavior points to a particular developmental issue, you need to work with the child's parents, other caregivers who directly care for the child, and specialists (if necessary) to determine the causes of the problem and to create an individualized plan for working with the child in child care, with support from the parents at home.

Conclusion

The suggestions in this guide for practicing culturally responsive care-giving may seem overwhelming. It is not easy to change the way one acts, especially in an area as complicated as this one is. Remember the opening lines from *I Am Freedom's Child*: "We need all the different kinds of people we can find to make freedom's dream come true. So as I learn to like the differences in me, I learn to like the differences in you." If we want all children to experience the dream (or at least come closer to it than people have so far), the time and energy we put into becoming more culturally responsive caregivers are worthwhile.

Remind yourself of an experience you enjoyed that involved a cultural difference between you and another person.

Note the experience here.

What do you feel you gained?

Why was it enjoyable?

Share your experience with another staff person.

Thinking/Doing Activity 2

What strengths do you bring to developing culturally responsive caregiving practices?

Check the ones you feel you already have:

- ❏ Curiosity about others

- ❏ Enjoyment of others

- ❏ Willingness to learn from mistakes

- ❏ Willingness to take risks

- ❏ Sense of humor

- ❏ Creativity

- ❏ Flexibility

- ❏ Commitment

Add others you believe are important.

Thinking/Doing Activity 3

What makes you uncomfortable about learning to be more culturally responsive?

What is the worst thing you can imagine might happen?

Write down your thoughts.

Discuss them with other caregivers.

Write down your feelings about the ratings of the three responses to Scenario 1: A Baby Crying.

Discuss the three responses with other caregivers who have done the writing activity. Discuss each person's feelings about the ratings of the three responses.

Thinking/Doing Activity 5

This activity can be done with scenarios 1, 2, or 3. Begin this activity by reading one of the scenarios.

Has your center or family child care home faced a similar problem?

If so, what did you do?

Would you still solve the problem in the same way?

If the situation arose in the future, with which solution would you feel comfortable?

Write down situations of cultural differences that have occurred in your child care setting.

Use the situations to role-play with other caregivers; then analyze culturally repressive and culturally responsive ways to handle cultural issues.

References

Martin, Bill, Jr. *I Am Freedom's Child.* Glendale, Calif.: Bowmar Publishing Co., 1970.

Suggested Resources

Alike and Different: Exploring Our Humanity with Young Children (Revised edition). Edited by Bonnie Neugebauer. Washington, D.C.: National Association for the Education of Young Children, 1992.

Provides insightful and useful discussions of important issues in working with parents and children from diverse cultural backgrounds. The focus is on parents of preschool-age children, but the concepts are equally applicable to infants and toddlers. For caregivers, directors, and trainers.

Carter, Margie. "Honoring Diversity: Problems and Possibilities for Staff and Organization," in *Alike and Different: Exploring Our Humanity with Young Children* (Revised edition). Edited by Bonnie Neugebauer. Washington, D.C.: National Association for the Education of Young Children, 1992, pp. 70–81.

Discusses how to create an environment that supports staff in learning to be culturally responsive. For caregivers and directors.

Cultural Perspectives on Child Development. Edited by Daniel A. Wagner and Harold W. Stevenson. San Francisco: W. H. Freeman and Co., 1981.

Provides theoretical and research insights into the impact of cultural context on infants' development. See the following articles: C. Super and S. Harkness, "The Development of Affect in Infancy and Early Childhood" (pp. 1–20); B. Lester and T. B. Brazelton, "Cross-Cultural Assessment of Neonatal Behavior" (pp. 20–54); and "Culture and the Language of Socialization: Parental Speech" (pp. 54–77). For trainers.

Derman-Sparks, Louise, and the A. B. C. Task Force. *Anti-Bias Curriculum: Tools for Empowering Young Children.* Washington, D.C.: National Association for the Education of Young Children, 1989.

Presents concrete reasons and ideas for creating inclusive, nonstereotyped child care environments. See especially Chapter 1, "Why Anti-bias Curriculum" (pp. 1–10); Chapter 2, "Creating an Anti-bias Environment" (pp. 11–20); Chapter 3, "Beginnings: Working with Two-year-olds" (pp. 21–30); and "Resources: Children's Books and Curriculum Materials" (pp. 119–36). For caregivers, directors, and trainers.

France, P. "Working with Young Bilingual Children," *Early Child Development and Care*, Vol. 10 (1980), 283–92.

Explores basic concepts of the impact of culture on Latino preschool children's learning and language development. Readers can apply the concepts to the infants and toddlers in their care. For caregivers, directors, and trainers.

Kitano, Margie K. "Early Childhood Education for Asian American Children," *Young Children,* Vol. 35 (January, 1980), 13–26.

Explores basic concepts of the impact of culture on Asian American preschool children's learning. Readers can apply the concepts to the infants and toddlers in their care. For caregivers, directors, and trainers.

McCracken, J. "Tossed Salad Is Terrific: Values of Multicultural Programs for Children and Families," in *Alike and Different: Exploring Our Humanity with Young Children* (Revised edition). Edited by Bonnie Neugebauer. Washington, D.C.: National Association for the Education of Young Children, 1992, pp. 92–97.

Gives concrete examples of providing culturally sensitive child care. For caregivers and directors.

Neugebauer, Bonnie. "What Are We Really Saying to Children? Criteria for the Selection of Books and Materials," in *Alike and Different: Exploring Our Humanity with Young Children* (Revised edition). Edited by Bonnie Neugebauer. Washington, D.C.: National Association for the Education of Young Children, 1992, pp. 160–62.

Offers a short, excellent checklist for evaluating the diversity of a program's books, materials, and equipment. For caregivers, directors, and trainers.

Powell, Douglas R. *Families and Early Childhood Programs*. Washington, D.C.: National Association for the Education of Young Children, 1989.

Presents an excellent discussion of current research for trainers. See especially Chapter 2, "From the Perspective of Children: Continuity Between Families and Early Childhood Programs" (pp. 23–49), on why culturally responsive practices are important; Chapter 3, "From the Perspective of Adults: Relations Between Parents and Early Childhood Programs" (pp. 53–85); and Chapter 4, "Parent Education and Support: Program Processes and Effects" (pp. 89–102). Chapters 3 and 4 discuss current knowledge about what does and does not lead to effective parent-staff relationships. For caregivers and directors.

Rashid, Hakim M. "Promoting Biculturalism in Young African-American Children," *Young Children*, Vol. 39 (January, 1984), 12–23.

Explores basic concepts of the impact of culture on African-American preschool children's learning. Readers can apply the concepts to the infants and toddlers in their care. For caregivers, directors, and trainers.

Raymond, G., and D. McIntosh. "The Impact of Current Changes in Social Structure on Early Childhood Education Programs," in *Alike and Different: Exploring Our Humanity with Young Children* (Revised edition). Edited by Bonnie Neugebauer. Washington, D.C.: National Association for the Education of Young Children, 1992, pp. 116–26.

Discusses changing family forms (styles) and economic realities and what early childhood programs must do to support all families. For caregivers, directors, and trainers.

West, B. "Children Are Caught Between Home and School, Culture and School," in *Alike and Different: Exploring Our Humanity With Young Children* (Revised edition). Edited by Bonnie Neugebauer. Washington, D.C.: National Association for the Education of Young Children, 1992, pp. 124–36.

Explores how a program's activities or expectations may conflict with family beliefs and suggests ways to handle the conflict. For caregivers, directors, and trainers.

Creating an Inclusive, Nonstereotypical Environment for Infants and Toddlers

Louise Derman-Sparks

Knowledge is incomplete about the process of identity awareness in children during the first two years of life. Nevertheless, infants and toddlers are continually absorbing the sights and sounds of the environments that surround them, and the relationship they have with the people who care for them transmits important messages about their identity and about values and ways of living. By two years of age, children begin to verbalize an interest in gender differences and noticeable physical characteristics of people, such as skin color and hair texture and color. Thus, although ethnic attributes of people may not yet be especially meaningful to infants and toddlers, they are likely to begin noticing differences among people. The materials you put in your child care environment provide young children with important data about what you consider to be true and valuable about people.

A diversity-rich, stereotype-free visual and auditory environment provides the sights and sounds that young children use to begin developing positive self-awareness and comfortable relationships with others. All child care environments must reflect the rich variety between and within cultural and ethnic groups. Every adult has the responsibility to ensure that:

1. Every child in the program is represented visually.

2. The diversity in the United States is represented.

3. No stereotypical or insulting images of any group are present.

Caregivers must thoughtfully evaluate every picture, mobile, book, doll, manipulative toy, and so forth that they offer to children. The following are some guidelines to help you evaluate and improve your environment:

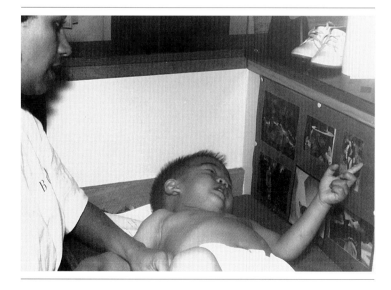

Visual Environment

- Provide an abundance of images of *all* the children, families, and staff in your program. Photographs and other pictures reflecting the various backgrounds of the children and staff should be attractively displayed.
- If the classroom population is racially or ethnically homogeneous, provide images of children and adults from the major racial and ethnic groups in your community and in U.S. society at large.
- Make sure the images accurately reflect people's current daily lives in the United States, both at work and with their families during recreational activities.
- Create numerical balance among different groups. Make sure people of color are not represented as tokens—that is, only one or two images among many other images.
- Provide a fair balance of images of women and men doing jobs both in and outside the home. Show women and men doing blue-collar work (e.g., factory worker, repair person) and pink-collar work (e.g., beautician, salesperson) as well as white-collar work (e.g., teacher, doctor).
- Show images of elderly people of various backgrounds doing different activities.
- Include images of people with disabilities (of various backgrounds) doing work and enjoying recreational activities with their families. Be careful not to use images that depict people with disabilities as dependent and passive.
- Provide images of diversity in family styles: single mothers or fathers, extended families, families in which one parent and a grandparent are the only adults, interracial and multiethnic families, adopted families, families in which a member has a disability (either a child or a parent), and other family configurations.

Books

- Provide picture books that reflect diversity of gender roles, different racial and cultural backgrounds, various special needs and abilities, a range of occupations, and a range of ages.

- Present accurate images and information (watch out for the "I is for Indian" stereotypical image in many alphabet books).
- Show people from all groups living their daily lives—working, being with family, solving issues relevant to young children, and having celebrations. Most books should be about contemporary life in the United States.
- Depict a variety of children and families within a group by having several books that represent a culture.
- Depict various family lifestyles and different socioeconomic levels and religions.

- Provide staff-made picture books about each child, with four or five photographs of the child doing her or his favorite activities.
- Make picture books with themes like "all kinds of babies" or "all kinds of families" (use autograph-size photo albums) (Derman-Sparks 1989).

Dramatic Play

At about fifteen to eighteen months of age, toddlers show interest in the beginnings of pretend play. The activity is an important developmental step in their learning how to create symbols (representing absent objects and imitating actions of others in play), a step that eventually leads to learning how to read. To support pretend play:

- Provide dolls that accurately reflect different racial/ethnic identities and physical abilities and both genders, including anatomically correct dolls. A variety of dolls enables young children to gain familiarity and ease with diver-

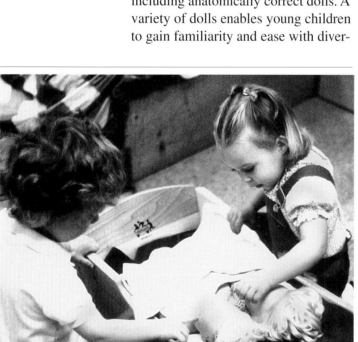

sity. The teacher puts the dolls in the classroom; the children invent the activities. You can make dolls by using patterns found in sewing books or with help from someone you know who makes dolls. Make cloth dolls of different skin colors and shades, hair texture, and eye color; make dolls with different physical abilities: a doll in a wheelchair, with braces, with a hearing aid, or with a seeing-eye dog. Be sure your special-needs dolls reflect various racial and ethnic backgrounds.
- Provide hats and clothing worn by men and women, a variety of props that reflect blue-collar as well as white-collar work, and kitchen implements from different ethnic groups.
- Display pictures in the housekeeping area that show families from several racial and ethnic backgrounds, family members with disabilities, different kinds of family organization (e.g., single-parent and extended families), and women and men doing a variety of household tasks.
- Support children's exploration of nonstereotypical gender roles. Intervene when a child tells another child that she or he cannot do something because the child is a girl or a boy. Help boys get involved in dramatic play.
- Include a few full-length mirrors in the housekeeping center. Occasionally, when two or three children are playing there, ask them questions about their skin, eye, and hair color as they look at each other in the mirror (Derman-Sparks 1989).

Art Materials

- Regularly provide brown and black tempera, finger paints, crayons, magic markers, colored chalk, easel paper, drawing paper, and paper for pasting.

- Frequently provide play dough in a spectrum of skin colors from light to dark.
- Frequently mix tempera in different skin shades for easel painting.
- Display artwork—prints, sculpture, textiles—by artists of various backgrounds, reflecting the aesthetic environment and culture of the families represented in your classroom and of groups in your community and in the United States (*Alike and Different* 1992; Derman-Sparks 1989).

Blocks, Trucks, and Small People Figures

- Make sure small people figures include men and women from a variety of racial and ethnic backgrounds.
- Regularly observe which children use the blocks and trucks. Make sure girls get a turn to use those materials (Derman-Sparks 1989).

Language

The environment should provide numerous opportunities for children to see and hear their home language. Examples include labels on materials (e.g., blocks and puzzles), alphabet and number posters, alphabet and simple picture books, songs, and finger games (Derman-Sparks 1989).

Cameras

A Polaroid or regular color camera is an invaluable tool for creating diversity-rich, stereotype-free materials for your child care program. Use the camera to take photographs of children, staff, and families. Mount the photographs at the children's eye level in the room and use photographs to make posters, mobiles, placemats, cubby labels, simple puzzles, and simple picture books.

Sources of Diverse Materials

Finding nonstereotyped materials about various groups is not always easy, even in large cities with more access to

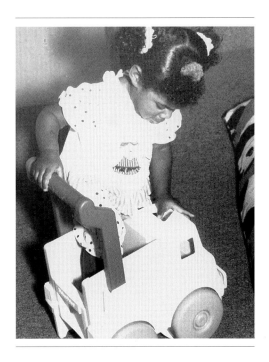

educational materials. Making your own materials to supplement commercial ones is essential. With ingenuity, creativity, patience, resourcefulness, and a little help from parents and friends, you can make wonderful materials.

Develop a picture file. Keep your eyes open for good pictures wherever you go. Some helpful resources include the following:

1. Magazines, such as *Young Children, Pre-K Today, Ms, Ebony, Life,* and *Essence;* Lakeshore materials catalog; and UNICEF appointment books.

2. Calendars made by organizations that work on diversity issues, such as UNICEF, National Black Child Development Institute, Syracuse Peace Workers, and women's movement groups.

3. Posters. The National Association for the Education of Young Children has excellent, inexpensive posters. Good posters are also often available from organizations in your community that are concerned with rights for children, women, ethnic minority groups, and people with disabilities.

Creating a diversity-rich, stereotype-free environment will take some effort. But once you have begun, the task will get easier. Remember that your children deserve a supportive environment.

References

Alike and Different: Exploring Our Humanity with Young Children (Revised edition). 1992. Edited by Bonnie Neugebauer. Washington, D.C.: National Association for the Education of Young Children.

Derman-Sparks, Louise, and the A.B.C. Task Force. 1989. *Anti-Bias Curriculum: Tools for Empowering Young Children.* Washington, D.C.: National Association for the Education of Young Children.

Supporting Staff Relationships in a Culturally Responsive Program

Louise Derman-Sparks

For caregivers to provide culturally responsive caregiving in group care settings, the relationships among the caregivers must also be culturally responsive. A safe emotional climate that recognizes cultural diversity and gives adults permission to ask questions, to learn from their mistakes, and to learn from each other is essential. Creating that safety is everyone's responsibility—it can happen only if every staff member cooperates in the effort. Ensuring a safe, supportive climate is an ongoing task for which the director of a program must provide leadership.

In "Honoring Diversity: Problems and Possibilities for Staff and Organization" (Carter 1992, 70–81), Margie Carter offers some helpful suggestions. Material from Carter's article is presented here. The article is written for caregivers in centers, but the same principles apply to family child care providers in their relationships with parents and colleagues.

Building Cohesiveness in the Midst of Diversity

As diversity on a staff increases, so do the possible problem areas. Continual work must be done to build group consensus and a team spirit. We must take care not to assume that everyone sees things in the same way, and we must take time to discover, appreciate, and learn from our differences. In doing so, we will recognize that both family backgrounds and cultural beliefs and practices influence the assumptions and behaviors we have acquired.

In her book titled *Teaching Adults: An Active Learning Approach,* Elizabeth Jones [1986] discusses methods she has used to help teachers become aware of what influences their own development in order to better understand their work in the child development field. She asks people to look over a list of characteristics used to describe an *ideal child*. First they are to check the characteristics that

The sections titled "Building Cohesiveness in the Midst of Diversity" and "Staff Agreements and Approaches to Criticism When Agreements Are Broken" are excerpted from Margie Carter, "Honoring Diversity: Problems and Possibilities for Staff and Organization," in *Alike and Different: Exploring Our Humanity with Young Children* (Revised edition). Edited by Bonnie Neugebauer. Washington, D.C.: National Association for the Education of Young Children, 1992, pp. 75–77 and 78–79, respectively. Used by permission of the author.

indicate the kind of person their parents wanted them to become and to cross off those characteristics considered undesirable and usually discouraged or punished. They then repeat the process, indicating the kind of person they would like their child to become. This exercise provokes passionate discussion and deeper insights into oneself and one's coworkers.

On other occasions Jones has concluded a brief lecture introducing the concept of culture by asking those in the group who can confidently name their culture to stand up and do so. The rest of the group then joins those standing, forming small cluster groups to identify the different beliefs and behaviors of each culture named. This exercise helps teachers to distinguish fact from fiction in cultural stereotypes and also to uncover the discrepancies that occur between beliefs and behaviors. Incorporating such activities into our staff meetings will help us get to know ourselves and each other better. We may also clarify changes we want to make to overcome any acquired biases or behaviors that we don't want to pass along to the children in our care.

Regular staff meetings are essential for communication and decision making in diverse groups. Without them routine concerns can become a major source of tension. I remember well a center discussion on whether to have a policy requiring the children to eat all of their food before leaving the table. One teacher said, "My family always used the line about the poor, starving Chinese, and I hated it." Another added, "We were never forced to eat anything in my family, and I think that has limited my acquired tastes." Almost under her breath a third voice said, "We just hoped there was enough food on the table when I was growing up." Almost by accident this staff discussion uncovered these dramatically different experiences influencing our views. It deepened our understanding and appreciation of each other and caused us to draw closer together as a staff. From there we were able to more objectively discuss what message we wanted to convey to the children and to set our policy accordingly.

On another occasion the staff took up the question of what the center should do for Halloween. One teacher explained that the more she was reading about the historic role of witches as midwives, healers, and mediators in primitive cultures, the more uncomfortable she felt with the Halloween stereotype of witches as wicked and evil. "It's like blaming the victim. These women were burned at the stake by the thousands for their beliefs and practices." Another teacher spoke up, "In my church we are told not to celebrate Halloween because it is a pagan practice based on demons and sin. I've always hated it for that reason." Because the goal of the discussion was to explore and understand, the thinking of each of us was broadened by hearing these differing views. We created a Halloween party that centered on the lesson that it is not only fun but instructive to pretend to be some-one you really aren't—learning what life is like behind that mask.

Each of these examples could have been occasions for staff conflicts, divisions, and tensions, but instead we used them to bring us closer together across our differences. This happened not only because of the value we placed on diversity but because of the concrete way we provided for staff discussions, using active listening and problem-solving practices.

Things, of course, do not always go this smoothly. With the demands and stresses of child care work, staff tensions can mount to an intense level. To prevent things from deteriorating into personality conflicts or duplicities, we need a reference point against which we can test our assumptions and standards regarding acceptable staff behaviors. Such standards, along with a statement of how conflicts will be handled, should be included in written personnel policies if not in staff contracts.

Ideally, these expectations and approaches to conflict resolution will parallel what we have set out for the children in our program. For instance, a statement might read: "At our center we all share in caring for each other and for the environment. When someone forgets or breaks this agreement, we remind them of how it hurts the group, explore why this happened, and work together to help the person get back on track. We work out disagreements by taking turns listening carefully to each other, explaining what we understand, and exploring what changes are possible and acceptable to those involved."

Over the years our staff developed a paper called "Staff Agreements and Approaches to Criticism When Agreements Are Broken" [see accompanying box]. These agreements proved invaluable in helping us prevent unproductive criticisms based on subjective opinions or preferences. The investigative aspect countered the human tendency to become judgmental or defensive during a conflict.

Staff Agreements and Approaches to Criticism When Agreements Are Broken

1. We will each have an attitude of flexibility and cooperation in our work here, thinking of the needs of others and the group as a whole, along with our own needs.
2. We will each carry a full share of the workload, which includes some extra hours outside our work schedule (i.e., parent-teacher conferences, meetings, planning and preparation of activities, recordkeeping, progress reports).
3. We will each communicate directly and honestly with each other. We will be respectful and honorable in our interactions.
4. When problems or difficulties related to our work arise, we will address them rather than ignore or avoid them.
5. We will all be informed of significant problems that affect the center. These will be communicated in person as soon as possible and in writing as necessary.
6. We understand that it is appropriate to seek help from the director on sensitive or difficult issues.
7. When necessary, we will use a criticism/self-criticism discussion process to identify attitudes and behaviors that are negatively affecting our agreements.

Criticism/Self-Criticism Process

[We use this process] to investigate and educate so we continue to adhere to our agreements.

Questions to ask oneself before giving a criticism:

1. Is my criticism based on investigation or on assumption?

2. What is the most important element of the criticism? Secondary?

3. What is my side of the problem, my responsibility, or my contribution to it?

4. What are my disguises that keep me from being criticized?

5. Is my criticism intended to hurt or attack, or is it to educate?

6. How are our agreements hurt or helped by what I am criticizing?

7. How can I play a concrete, positive role in helping the other person change?

8. What changes do I need to make in myself?

Stating a criticism:

When you do . . .

I feel . . .

It hurts our agreements because . . .

Therefore I want you to . . .

In the future I will behave differently by . . .

Investigative discussion of the criticism:

Why do you feel that way? What happened?

What other things were going on (objective things happening; subjective impressions, feelings)?

What is the main thing that needed to happen here?

[See Thinking/Doing Activity 7 on page 73.]

References

Carter, Margie. 1992. "Honoring Diversity: Problems and Possibilities for Staff and Organization," in *Alike and Different: Exploring Our Humanity with Young Children* (Revised edition). Edited by Bonnie Neugebauer. Washington, D.C.: National Association for the Education of Young Children, pp. 70–81.

Jones, Elizabeth. 1986. *Teaching Adults: An Active Learning Approach.* Washington, D.C.: National Association for the Education of Young Children.

Now that you have read the rules created by one child care center staff, think about what would help you feel more comfortable in learning and using culturally responsive practices. Would you change or add new rules? Write down your list of rules for being culturally responsive to other staff. Consider what would help you feel free to do the following:

- **Acknowledge** what you do not know or a mistake you made.

- **Ask** parents and other staff for the information you need to better understand a child or family.

- **Adapt** or change your behavior to fit the needs of a child and his or her family.

Compare your list with other staff members' lists.
Agree on a common list for your center.

Section Four:
Suggested Resources

Suggested Resources

Books

Alike and Different: Exploring Our Humanity with Young Children (Revised edition). Edited by Bonnie Neugebauer. Washington, D.C.: National Association for the Education of Young Children, 1992.

Explores the unique qualities that make us individuals; considers differences of physical and intellectual ability, economic situation, cultural heritage, sex, and age. For caregivers, directors, and trainers.

Beginning Equal: A Manual About Non-Sexist Childrearing for Infants and Toddlers. Edited by Merle Froschel and Barbara Sprung. Translated by Victoria Ortiz. New York: Women's Action Alliance, Inc., 1983.

Contains excellent suggestions for a nonsexist environment and for activities with infants and toddlers and excellent methods for parent workshops on a variety of gender/nonsexist issues. For trainers and directors.

Books Without Bias: Through Indian Eyes (Second edition). Edited by Beverly Slapin and Doris Seale. Berkeley, Calif.: Oyate, 1988.

Presents excellent critiques of how Native Americans are portrayed in children's books and offers many suggestions for selecting accurate books. Includes excellent essays and guidelines for evaluating all other materials and activities used in early childhood education to teach about Native Americans. For caregivers, directors, and trainers.

Culture and Childrearing. Edited by Ann L. Clark. Philadelphia: F. A. Davis, Co., 1981.

Focuses on assisting health professionals bring greater sensitivity to their practice. Explores the role of family members, child-rearing practices, infancy and early childhood, and other topics in a variety of cultural groups. For directors and trainers.

Derman-Sparks, Louise, and the A.B.C. Task Force. *Anti-Bias Curriculum: Tools for Empowering Young Children.* Washington, D.C.: National Association for the Education of Young Children, 1989.

Outlines an educational philosophy as well as specific techniques and content for implementing an anti-bias curriculum. Emphasizes the value of differences and asks teachers and children to confront troublesome issues rather than ignore them or cover them up. For directors and trainers.

Developing Cross-Cultural Competence: A Guide for Working with Young Children and Their Families. Edited by Eleanor W. Lynch and Marci J. Hanson. Baltimore, Md.: Paul H. Brookes Publishing Co., 1992.

Examines the role that culture plays in families' and professionals' beliefs, values, and behaviors. Explores the difficulties in adapting to a different culture. Provides strategies for effective cross-cultural interactions with families of young children who have or may be at risk of a disability or chronic illness. Offers an in-depth examination of families whose roots are Anglo-European, Native American, African American, Latino, Asian, Pilipino, native Hawaiian, Samoan, and Middle Eastern. For teachers, directors, and trainers.

Diversity and Developmentally Appropriate Practices: Challenges for Early Childhood Education. Edited by Bruce L. Mallory and Rebecca S. New. New York: Teachers College Press, Teachers College, Columbia University, 1994.

Offers critiques of early childhood education and developmentally appropriate practices. Seeks to expand the current definition of developmentally appropriate practices to include alternative theoretical and practical perspectives for addressing the needs of young children with cultural and developmental differences. For teachers, directors, and trainers.

Gibbs, Jewelle T., and Larke N. Huang. *Children of Color: Psychological Interventions with Minority Youth.* San Francisco: Jossey-Bass, Inc., Pubs., 1989.

Presents comprehensive guidelines for the assessment and treatment of minority children and adolescents from several cultures. Offers intervention strategies sensitive to cultural expectations, linguistic differences, and family structures. For directors and trainers.

Gonzalez-Mena, Janet. *The Child in the Family and the Community.* New York: Macmillan Publishing Co., 1993.

Examines the developmental context of socialization, providing information about the foundations of socialization and exploring four major issues of the first five years (attachment, autonomy, initiative, and self-esteem). Looks at the socialization of the child in a family context and in a community context.

Gonzalez-Mena, Janet. *Multicultural Issues in Child Care.* Mountain View, Calif.: Mayfield Publishing Co., 1993.

Focuses on cultural differences relevant to all caregiving settings. Emphasizes the importance of respect for cultural pluralism. Offers strategies for increasing caregivers' sensitivity to different cultural child care practices and values and for improving communication and understanding between the caregiver and parent. For caregivers, directors, and trainers.

Gonzalez-Mena, Janet, and Dianne W. Eyer. *Infants, Toddlers, and Caregivers* (Third, revised edition). Mountain View, Calif.: Mayfield Publishing Co., 1992.

Discusses the importance of addressing cultural differences in all aspects of the program. Emphasizes that caregivers should accept the parents' ways of doing things as much as possible and try to carry out their wishes. For caregivers, directors, and trainers.

Katz, P. "Development of Children's Racial Awareness and Intergroup Attitudes," in *Current Topics in Early Childhood Education.* Vol. 4. Edited by Lilian G. Katz. Norwood, N.J.: Ablex Publishing Corp., 1982, pp. 17–54.

Describes the overlapping but separable steps that occur in the acquisition of racial beliefs and sets a framework for growth throughout early childhood. For trainers.

Kendall, Frances E. *Diversity in the Classroom: A Multicultural Approach to the Education of Young Children.* New York: Teachers College Press, Teachers College, Columbia University, 1983.

Sets forth the author's philosophy that "children have the right to experience an affirmation of individual differences and a respect for the cultural heritages of all people." Presents strategies teachers can use to examine their own attitudes and values and to communicate a multicultural approach to parents. The information presented on each culture might be useful for early child care professionals working with children and families from those cultural groups. For caregivers, directors, and trainers.

McCracken, Janet Brown. *Valuing Diversity: The Primary Years.* Washington, D.C.: National Association for the Education of Young Children, 1993.

Emphasizes the importance of learning to value and find strength in each other's diversity—to appreciate the different ways in which others live and teach. Offers strategies for examining one's beliefs and values and for helping children to value diversity. Suggests resources for further exploration of the ideas presented by the author. For teachers, directors, and trainers.

Ramsey, Patricia G. *Teaching and Learning in a Diverse World: Multicultural Education for Young Children.* New York: Teachers College Press, Teachers College, Columbia University, 1987.

Explores how early childhood educators can deal with the problems of prejudice relating to race, culture, socioeconomic status, and gender. Presents information for teachers to consider when examining and analyzing their values and perspectives. For directors and trainers.

Slapin, Beverly. *Books Without Bias: A Guide to Evaluating Children's Literature for Handicapism* (Second edition). San Francisco: Squeaky Wheels Press, 1990.

Offers wonderful critiques of numerous books and is a useful guide for evaluating photographs, posters, and magazine pictures about people with disabilities. For caregivers, directors, and trainers.

Periodicals

Booth-Butterfield, Melanie. "The Cues We Don't Question: Unintentional Gender Socialization in the Day Care Facility," *Day Care and Early Education,* Vol. 8 (Summer, 1981), 20–22.

Describes the many ways in which caregivers unawarely treat boys and girls differently and teach gender-stereotyped behavior. For caregivers, directors, and trainers.

France, P. "Working with Young Bilingual Children," *Early Child Development and Care,* Vol. 10 (1980), 283–92.

Explores basic concepts of the impact of culture on Latino preschool children's learning and language development. Readers can apply the concepts to the infants and toddlers in their care. For caregivers, directors, and trainers.

George, Felicia. "Checklist for a Non-Sexist Classroom," *Young Children,* Vol. 45 (January, 1990), 10–11.

Can serve as a model for cultural and ethnic issues as well as nonsexism. Gender bias is another important consideration in planning appropriate programs and providing sensitive care for infants and toddlers. For caregivers, directors, and trainers.

Kitano, Margie K. "Early Childhood Education for Asian American Children," *Young Children,* Vol. 35 (January, 1980), 13–26.

Explores basic concepts of the impact of culture on Asian American pre-school children's learning. Readers can apply the concepts to the infants and toddlers in their care. For caregivers, directors, and trainers.

Morrow, Robert D. "What's in a Name? In Particular, a Southeast Asian Name?" *Young Children,* Vol. 44 (September, 1989), 20–23.

Describes the importance of a person's name in various Southeast Asian cultures, especially the Vietnamese, Cambodian, Laotian, and Hmong cultures. Gives readers practical suggestions about children and their names. For caregivers, directors, and trainers.

Phillips, Carol B. "Nurturing Diversity for Today's Children and Tomorrow's Leaders," *Young Children,* Vol. 43 (January, 1988), 42–47.

Discusses the inequities in American society toward people of color. Focuses on four major strategies that caregivers and educators can use in providing equity to all groups in their programs for young children. For caregivers, directors, and trainers.

Rashid, Hakim M. "Promoting Biculturalism in Young African-American Children," *Young Children,* Vol. 39 (January, 1984), 12–23.

Explores basic concepts of the impact of culture on African American pre-school children's learning. Readers can apply the concepts to the infants and toddlers in their care. For caregivers, directors, and trainers.

Schon, I. "Hispanic Books/Libros Hispanicos," *Young Children,* Vol. 42 (May, 1988), 81–85.

Provides an excellent resource guide for caregivers. The first part of the article recommends resource books for adults seeking to develop Hispanic literature collections for children. The second section annotates specific children's books in Spanish. Includes a list of U.S. dealers of books in Spanish and a bibliography for further reading. For caregivers, directors, and trainers.

Sheldon, Amy. " 'Kings Are Royaler Than Queens': Language and Socialization," *Young Children,* Vol. 45 (January, 1990), 4–9.

Discusses how "our language reflects sexist, male-centered attitudes that perpetuate the trivialization, marginalization, and invisibility of female experience in our country." Like the "Checklist for a Non-Sexist Classroom," the article shows how issues of culture, race, and ethnicity are handled inappropriately in American society. Helps one think about and become more conscious of the bias in this country and how that bias seriously impacts all children and families. For caregivers, directors, and trainers.

Wardle, Francis. "Are You Sensitive to Interracial Children's Special Identity

Needs?" *Young Children,* Vol. 42 (January, 1987), 53–59.

Focuses primarily on the issues affecting children from interracial families and discusses the role of the caregiver in supporting the child and the family. Includes a helpful national resource guide of groups serving interracial families and a list of appropriate books for interracial families. For caregivers, directors, and trainers.

Wardle, Francis. "Endorsing Children's Differences: Meeting the Needs of Adopted Minority Children," *Young Children,* Vol. 45 (July, 1990), 44–46.

Focuses on families who have adopted children from racial or ethnic groups other than their own and discusses how to promote the child's positive identity. For caregivers, directors, and trainers.

Organizations

California Department of Education (CDE), Bureau of Publications, Sales Unit, P.O. Box 271, Sacramento, CA 95812-0271; telephone (916) 445-1260.

Claudia's Caravan, 1918 Lafayette St., Alameda, CA 94501; telephone (510) 521-7871.

Claudia's Caravan sells multicultural anti-bias books and toys.

Cynthia's Educational Toys & Games, City Center Square, 501 14th St., Oakland, CA 94612; telephone (510) 464-3646.

Cynthia's stocks a range of multicultural books and toys.

Educational Equity Concepts, 114 E. 32nd St., New York, NY 10016; telephone (212) 725-1803.

The group is a national nonprofit organization founded in 1982 to foster equal educational opportunity. The organization designs innovative programs and materials to help eliminate bias based on sex, race, and disability; offers a broad range of training and consulting services; and engages in a variety of public education activities.

ERIC Clearinghouse on Elementary and Early Childhood Education, University of Illinois at Urbana-Champaign, 805 W. Pennsylvania Ave., Urbana, IL 61801.

ERIC offers a free newsletter with reviews of a wide variety of publications, including ERIC documents, digests, annotated resource lists, and computerized ready-searches. An annotated resource list, entitled "Multicultural Education for Young Children," is free on request.

Global Village, 2210 Wilshire Blvd., Suite 262, Santa Monica, CA 90403; telephone (213) 459-5188.

The organization specializes in multicultural antibias books, toys, and records.

Lomel Enterprises, Inc., P.O. Box 2452, Washington, DC 20013; telephone (202) 526-2949 and 526-1196.

The business sells authentic African American dolls and accessories.

National Center for Clinical Infant Program (NCCIP), 2000 14th St., North, Suite 380, Arlington, VA 22201-2500; telephone (703) 528-4300.

Two recent publications from NCCIP are related to culture:

Anderson, P., and E. S. Fenichel. *Serving Culturally Diverse Families of*

Infants and Toddlers with Disabilities (1989).

Zero to Three Bulletin, Vol. 10 (April, 1990). The entire issue is related to the impact of culture on infants and families.

Audiovisuals

America's Women of Color. Women's Educational Equity Act Publishing Center, Education Development Corporation, 55 Chapel St., Newton, MA 02610. Filmstrips.

Anti-bias Curriculum. Pacific Oaks Extension Services, 714 W. California Blvd., Pasadena, CA 91105. Videotape.

Black History: Lost, Stolen or Strayed. Kit Parker Films, 1245 Tenth St., Monterey, CA 93940-3692. Film.

Chinese Americans: Realities and Myths. Institute for Peace and Justice, 4144 Lindell, Rm. 122, St. Louis, MO 63108. Filmstrip.

Essential Connections: Ten Keys to Culturally Sensitive Care. California Department of Education, Bureau of Publications, Sales Unit, P.O. Box 271, Sacramento, CA 95812-0271; telephone (916) 445-1260. Videotape.

Frontline: A Class Divided. Public Broadcasting Service, 1320 Braddock Pl., Alexandria, VA 22314. Videotape.

Hispanic Heritage. National Public Radio, Customer Service, P.O. Box 55417, Madison, WI 53705. Cassette, order number VW-79-09-09.

The Japanese-American: Four Generations of Adaptation. National Public Radio, Customer Service, P.O. Box 55417, Madison, WI 53705. Cassettes, order number CR-79-08-17.

Japanese-Americans: An Inside Look. Japanese American Curriculum Project, 414 Third Ave., San Mateo, CA 94401. Filmstrip.

Native American Youth: The New Warriors. National Public Radio, Customer Service, P.O. Box 55417, Madison, WI 53705. Cassette, order number HO-80-11-26.

Not All Parents Are Straight. Full Frame Production, 363 Brannan St., San Francisco, CA 94107. Videotape.

Proverbs: Wit and Wisdom of Afro-Americans. National Public Radio, Customer Service, P.O. Box 55417, Madison, WI 53705. Cassette, order number HO-84-04-18.

Six Native American Families. Society for Visual Education, 1345 Diversey Pkwy., Chicago, IL 60614. Six filmstrips.

Women and Disability: The Issues. Educational Equity Concepts, 114 E. 32nd St., Third Floor, Rm. 306, New York, NY 10016. Videotape.

Women in American History. Educational Activities, Inc., P.O. Box 392, Freeport, NY 11520. Filmstrip.

Women on the March. National Film Board of Canada, 1251 Avenue of the Americas, New York, NY 10020. Film.

Appendix
Caregiver-Parent Information/Resources Forms

The following forms are included in this appendix:

- Parent Interview Form
- Infant/Toddler Child Care Enrollment Application
- Information for Daily Care
- Schedule Information

Each of the forms is intended to elicit child-rearing and developmental information from parents to help caregivers provide developmentally and culturally sensitive care for infants and toddlers. Therefore, numerous questions are asked about extended family members, home language, and child-rearing practices.

The initial communication between the caregiver and the family is vital to establishing a trusting relationship with parents. With a respectful and informative approach in your communication with the families about the importance of the information you seek, you will gain valuable insights about the family and its cultural practices. The process by which the information is gained is as important as the information itself.

The use of forms as part of a caregiver's initial communication with families has been alluded to in several chapters in this guide. The forms in this appendix are intended only as samples; you should modify them to meet *your* caregiving situation.

Parent Interview Form

Child's name: _____ Date of birth: _____ Sex: _____

Nickname(s) child responds to: _____

Date of admission: _____ Age: _____

Parent(s) interviewed: _____

Interviewed by: _____ Date: _____

_____

1. Reason for choosing child care for your child:

2. Family relationships:
   a. What is the mother's responsibility in the family (including work, school, other responsibilities)?

   b. What is the father's responsibility in the family (including work, school, other responsibilities)?

   c. Relationships with brothers and sisters:

   Name of sibling(s)   *Age*   *If not living at home, where located*

   _____

   _____

   _____

   _____

d. Relationships with others living in the home (not parents or siblings):

Name	Age	*Relationship to child*	*Does the person take care of the child? How often?*

3. What is the primary language spoken in the home? _____

    Mother's primary language? _____

    Father's primary language? _____

4. What sounds or words does your child use to communicate his/her needs?

5. If your child is in diapers, do you use:

    Powder? _____   Ointment? _____

    Other? _____

    Is your child allergic to disposable diapers? _____

6. If your child uses the toilet, please describe how you know when he/she needs to use it; what words he/she uses when he/she asks to use the toilet.

7. Does your child have strong likes or dislikes in food?

    a. What is a regular mealtime like in your home?

    b. Any food allergies?

8. How does your child nap at home?

    a. At what times does your child usually nap?

    b. Approximately how long is your child's nap?

    c. Where does your child usually nap?

    d. Does he/she have any special "cuddly" or blanket?

    e. Does your child sleep on his/her back? stomach?

    f. If there are problems about sleeping, do you have any special way of handling them?

9. Characteristics of emotional behavior:

    a. How does he/she express feelings of pleasure, excitement, or joy?

    b. How does he/she express anger, react to frustration?

    c. What helps make your child feel better when he/she is upset?

    d. How does your child feel about being separated from parents?

    e. Has your child experienced any long separations from parents?

    f. How does your child react to being cared for by people other than mother or father?

    g. Does your child have any fears, such as fear of animals or loud noises?

h. How does your child respond to being told no?

i. Does any of your child's behavior cause you concern? Are any behaviors a problem?

10. What are your child's play activities? List favorite toys:

11. In a few sentences, how would you describe your child?

12. Is there any other information concerning your child that would be helpful for us to know (e.g., hospitalization, injuries, need for special medication)?

Adapted with permission from the parent interview form developed by:

Preschool Mental Health Consultation Program
Early Childhood Mental Health Program
2801 Robert Miller Drive
Richmond, CA 94806

Modified by Louise Derman-Sparks and Carol Young-Holt, July, 1989.

Infant/Toddler Child Care Enrollment Application

Desired entry day: _____

Child's name: _____ Date of birth: _____ Girl: _____ Boy: _____

Nickname(s): _____

SHIFT: AM____ PM____ EVE____ WEEKENDS_____ HOURS _____

Mother's name: _____ Occupation: _____

Place of employment (name, address, telephone number and extension):

_____

_____

Hours and days of employment: _____

Home address: _____ Home telephone: _____

Father's name: _____ Occupation: _____

Place of employment (name, address, telephone number and extension):

_____

_____

Hours and days of employment: _____

Home address: _____ Home telephone: _____

Primary language spoken at home: Father: _____ Mother: _____

How do you describe your child's ethnicity? _____

Child lives with: Mother _____   Father _____   Both _____   Guardian _____

Siblings: Name and age

_____

_____

_____

Other persons living in home: Name, age, primary language, and relationship to child

_____

_____

_____

Other family members (describe): _____

_____

_____

Describe your child's general health, special needs, or allergies:

_____

_____

_____

_____

Are there special things you do to keep your child safe? _____

_____

_____

Describe whom you use for medical care: _____

_____

Describe your child's emotional characteristics or temperament: _____

_____

_____

Activities your child likes: _____

How does he/she spend his/her time? _____

_____

_____

What are your goals for your child at this time? _____

_____

_____

How do you discipline your child? _____

_____

_____

Does your child need any special care? _____

_____

_____

What do you do when your child does something you think is wrong or bad for your child or when your child does not listen to you? _____

_____

_____

Special information that we should know to serve your child better: _____

_____

_____

Are there any special holidays or occasions that you would like to celebrate with your child?

_____

_____

Has your child been cared for by people other than you? Yes _____ No _____

If yes, who has cared for your child? _____

_____

Other comments: _____

_____

_____

Adapted with permission from the form used by:

Huntington Memorial Hospital
Child Care Center
100 Congress Street
P.O. Box 7013
Pasadena, CA 91109-7013

Modified by Louise Derman-Sparks and Carol Lou Young-Holt for use as a sample enrollment form that deals with issues of culture, ethnicity, and primary language.

Information for Daily Care

Name of child   Date of birth   Today's date   Child's age today

FEEDING

Breast-fed: _____   Bottle-fed: _____

Formula milk: _____

Milk substitute: _____

Does your child like to eat? Explain: _____

_____

Frequency: _____

What food is he/she eating and how much:

Fruits: _____   Juices: _____

Vegetables: _____   Meats: _____

Cereals: _____   Eggs: _____

Who feeds your baby? _____

Does your child take vitamins/vitamins-minerals?

_____

Has your child been allergic to any food? _____

_____

Are there foods that your religion/your beliefs forbid eating? _____

_____

Do you feed your child? _____   How? _____

Does your child feed herself/himself? _____

SLEEPING

How do you put your child to sleep? _____

Where does your child sleep? _____

What kind of sleeper is your child? _____

Daytime naps: _____ How many naps? _____ How long are naps? _____

Nighttime sleep: _____

Does your child fuss or cry when going to sleep? _____

Does your child fuss or cry when waking up? _____

Does child sleep on his/her back? _____ Stomach? _____ Child's preference: _____

Special toy or blanket, etc., child is attached to: _____

_____

Special words for family, pets, etc.: _____

_____

DIAPERS

Cloth: _____ Disposable: _____

What do you do for diaper rash? _____

_____

How do you handle toileting? _____

What is child's word for bowel movement? _____

Urine? _____

CRYING

What do you do when your child cries? _____

_____

Adapted with permission from the form used by:

Huntington Memorial Hospital
Child Care Center
100 Congress Street
P.O. Box 7013
Pasadena, CA 91109-7013

Modified by Louise Derman-Sparks and Carol Lou Young-Holt for use as a sample enrollment form that deals with issues of culture, ethnicity, and primary language.

Schedule Information

Please give us your child's daily routine so that we may better care for her/him in the way that is most comfortable for you as a family.

We would like times and activities.

A.M.:

P.M.:

Bedtime:

_____   _____
Today's date   Name of child

Adapted with permission from the form used by:

    Huntington Memorial Hospital
    Child Care Center
    100 Congress Street
    P.O. Box 7013
    Pasadena, CA 91109-7013

Modified by Louise Derman-Sparks and Carol Lou Young-Holt for use as a sample enrollment form that deals with issues of culture, ethnicity, and primary language.

R00-091 002-4061-156 8/01 3,500